CONTENTS

I0695911

BIBLICAL SEXUALITY

What the Bible Teaches about
God's Purpose for our Sexuality

F. Wayne Mac Leod

Light To My Path Book Distribution

Copyright © 2018 F. Wayne Mac Leod

All rights reserved.

No part of this book may be reproduced or transmitted in any form or by any means without written permission of the author.

Scripture quotations marked (NIV) are taken from the Holy Bible, New International Version®, NIV®. Copyright © 1973, 1978, 1984, 2011 by Biblica, Inc.™ Used by permission of Zondervan. All rights reserved worldwide. www.zondervan.com The "NIV" and "New International Version" are trademarks registered in the United States Patent and Trademark Office by Biblica, Inc.™

"Scripture quotations marked (ESV) are from the ESV® Bible (The Holy Bible, English Standard Version®), copyright © 2001 by Crossway, a publishing ministry of Good News Publishers. Used by permission. All rights reserved."

Scripture quotations marked (NLT) are taken from the Holy Bible, New Living Translation, copyright ©1996, 2004, 2015 by Tyndale House Foundation. Used by permission of Tyndale House Publishers, Inc., Carol Stream, Illinois 60188. All rights reserved.

Scripture quotations from The Authorized (King James) Version. Rights in the Authorized Version in the United Kingdom are vested in the Crown. Reproduced by permission of the Crown's patentee, Cambridge University Press

PREFACE

It is never easy to write about such a private matter as human sexuality. I must admit that when the Lord put this on my heart, I struggled to commit to the topic. I have written this study, however, not only under the leading of the Lord, but because, as I watched what is happening around me, I felt it was time for the church to be reminded of God's purpose for our sexuality.

I recognize that what the Bible says on this topic is not popular. In fact, I could find myself in trouble by teaching what the Bible has to say about some of the issues covered in this study. It is my conviction, however, that the Bible is our standard for life and practice. Those who claim the name of Christ are called to live by the standards presented in this Word.

This is a survey of what the Bible teaches about human sexuality. My purpose is to lay out, in a compassionate way, what the Bible has to say about this important part of life. My prayer is that this effort will be a means of healing for some and a warning for others. I trust it will be a means by which God will speak to the lives and hearts of those who have been influenced by what our society is telling us. More than anything, however, I trust it will be a means by which the Spirit of God will reveal the purpose of God for a healthy and godly sexuality so that we again may know the fullness of His presence and blessing on our lives and society.

- F. Wayne Mac Leod

1 - THE CREATION OF MAN, WOMAN AND MARRIAGE

s we engage in this delicate topic, let's begin in Genesis with the story of creation.

26 Then God said, "Let us make man in our image, after our likeness. And let them have dominion over the fish of the sea and over the birds of the heavens and over the livestock and over all the earth and over every creeping thing that creeps on the earth." 27 So God created man in his own image, in the image of God he created him;
male and female he created them. (Genesis 1)

It is important to examine the Hebrew words used

in Genesis 1. Notice in verse 26 that God determined to make "man" in His own image. The word used for "man" is the Hebrew word adam from which we get the name of the first man. The word adam in the Hebrew language can refer to a man but it is often used to speak of humans in general whether they be male or female. In other words, Genesis 1:26 tells us that God decided to create human beings in His likeness.

Notice also in verse 27 that two kinds of humans were created. God created males and females. The word used for male in this verse is the Hebrew word *zakar* which clearly indicates a masculine gender. Unlike the word adam which may refer to male or female, *zakar* refers only to a male human or animal. The word used for female in Genesis 1:27 is also very exclusive. The word *neqebah* refers only to a female gender, whether human or animal.

Notice also in Genesis 1:28 that God not only created both male and female, but it was His intention that they be fruitful and multiply on the earth.

> *28 And God blessed them. And God said to them, "Be fruitful and multiply and fill the earth and subdue it, and have dominion over the fish of the sea and over the birds of the heavens and over every living thing that moves on the earth."*

To fulfil this purpose, both a male and female sex was required. God could have caused the earth to be populated in any number of ways, but this was His choice. The sexual union between a man and woman would be God's chosen method.

Genesis 1:31 tells us that when God examined the man and the woman he had made and His plan for the population of the earth, He proclaimed that everything was "very good."

31 And God saw everything that he had made, and behold, it was very good. And there was evening and there was morning, the sixth day. (Genesis 1)

In other words, it was exactly as He intended. Man, woman and the sexual union between them was holy and acceptable to Him –it was very good and would serve to accomplish His purpose for the population of the earth.

The creation of man and woman was so significant that Genesis 2 takes the time to go into further detail. Before the creation of woman, Adam, the first man, walked in the presence of God in the Garden of Eden. There in that garden, God placed animals of all kinds. In Genesis 2:18, however, we read:

> *18 Then the Lord God said, "It is not good that the man should be alone; I will make him a helper fit for him." (Genesis 2)*

Commenting on this, Jamieson, Faussett and Brown state:

> *It was not good for the man to be alone –in the midst of plenty and delights, he was conscious of feelings he could not gratify. (Jamieson, Robert; Fausset, A.R.; Brown, David; Commentary Critical and Explanatory on the Whole Bible: Laridian, 1871. Comments on Genesis 2:18)*

What is significant is that Adam, although he lived in the presence of God, still felt an emptiness in his heart. He was created with the need for a human helper and companion. God created him with this need. God also knew exactly what man needed to fill that need.

God determined that He would make a "helper fit for him" (Genesis 2:18). God decided to create a companion who was a perfect fit for Adam. She would be the solution to his loneliness.

It is important we understand that while Genesis 1 speaks about male and female being created with the purpose of multiplying and filling the earth, Genesis 2 speaks to this matter of Adam being "alone" and needing a companion or helper. The Hebrew word for helper used here is the word *ezer* which speaks of aid or assistance "whether material or immaterial" *(Baker, Warren; Carpenter, Eugene, AMG Word Study Dictionary, "Ezer h5828", Cedar Rapids, Laridian).*

The word "helper" therefore, does not just refer to the work that Adam had to do in the garden. Adam's needs were both "material" and "immaterial". In other words, he needed help in the practical matters of caring for the garden but also to deal with his loneliness. His needs were both physical and emotional in nature.

Genesis 2 goes on to tell us how God resolved Adam's need.

> *21 So the Lord God caused a deep sleep to fall upon the man, and while he slept took one of his ribs and closed up its place with flesh. 22 And the rib that the Lord God had taken from the man he made into a woman and brought her to the man. (Genesis 2)*

From Adam's rib, God created a woman. What is significant is the Hebrew word used in verse 22 for woman. The word *issah* can refer to a woman but more specifically to a wife. Notice also from verse 22 that the Lord God brought this woman (wife) to Adam. In other words, God presented Adam with a wife, who would be a helper to him and companion to him in his aloneness. This woman was God's response to Adam's need. She was created from him and for him particularly.

Woman and man were created for each other. The fact that God presented them to each other shows us that this was His purpose for their lives. They would minister to each other's needs (material and immaterial) and through them the earth would be populated.

Notice the response of Adam when God presented him with a wife:

> *23 Then the man said,*
> *"This at last is bone of my bones*
> *and flesh of my flesh;*
> *she shall be called Woman,*
> *because she was taken out of Man." (Genesis 2)*

Adam recognized that there was a very deep connection between himself and the wife God had given him. She came from him. Unlike the animals around him, the woman was part of him. She shared his nature. Through physically different from him, she was a perfect partner. He called her "woman" using the Hebrew term *issah* (wife) indicating the special relationship he had with her.

Adam would go on in verse 24 to speak a prophetic word revealing the purpose of God for marriage.

24 Therefore a man shall leave his father and his mother and hold fast to his wife, and they shall become one flesh.

Adam declares that a man would leave his parents and hold fast or be joined to his wife. The word Adam uses for "man" here is the Hebrew word *iys* which refers to a male but more specifically to a husband. The word is exclusively used for males. Adam is declaring here that a male husband would leave his father and mother and be joined together with his female wife. This is the clear meaning of the verse and the words used in this verse. Adam's words are prophetic in the sense that they proclaim the intention and purpose of God for marriage. Biblical marriage, as instituted by God in Genesis, is the union of a man and a woman.

For Consideration:

Why did God create both males and females?

Was the creation of males and females only to populate the earth?

God recognized that it was not good for man to be alone. Have you ever felt alone? What are some needs that being alone creates?

Why is Adam's statement in Genesis 2:24 significant? What does it tell us about the purpose of God for marriage?

If you are married, have you been the helper God intends you to be for your partner?

For Prayer:

Take a moment to thank the Lord that He understands our needs and is willing to minister to us in those needs.

If you are married ask the Lord to help you to be the partner He intended you to be for your husband or wife.

Ask the Lord to help us as a society and as believers to be true to Him and His purpose for marriage.

2 - MARRIAGE, SEXUALITY AND THE FALL

In the last chapter, we saw how God presented the first man with a wife. As we move to Genesis 3, we read about the fall of this first couple into sin. In the garden where they lived, was a tree with fruit that God had forbidden them to eat. Also, in that garden was their great enemy Satan. Disguising, himself as a serpent, Satan tempted Eve to eat from that forbidden tree. She surrendered to his temptations and disobeyed the command of God. She brought the fruit of the tree to her husband and he also ate and disobeyed the direct command of God (see Genesis 3:1-6).

This sin against God would change everything for Adam and Eve. Their relationship with the Creator and with each other would never again be the same.

From that point forward, every couple born into this world would suffer the effects of sin in their personal lives and relationships. The perfect relationship this first couple enjoyed in those early days would be no longer. Like an ugly disease, sin would ravage their marriage. Let's take a moment to consider the effects of sin on the relationship this first couple enjoyed.

In Genesis 3:7 we read:

7 Then the eyes of both were opened, and they knew that they were naked. And they sewed fig leaves together and made themselves loincloths.

It is striking that with the entrance of sin, one of the first things this first couple noticed was that they were naked. This was not new. From what we understand, they had been naked from the time of their creation and this was never an issue for them. With the entrance of sin, however, their nakedness became a problem. In fact, we read in Genesis 3:7 that their response was to sew fig leaves to hide their private parts from each other. Something changed the day sin entered the world. We are left to wonder what it was that caused this change of perspective.

The answer to this question comes in Genesis 3:10. Adam and Eve heard God walking in the garden. Genesis 3:8 tells us that their response was to hide from Him. God called out to them in Genesis 3:9 and asked them were they were. Listen to the response of Adam:

10 And he said, "I heard the sound of you in the garden, and I was afraid, because I was naked, and I hid myself."

Notice what Adam told God. He hid because he was afraid. He was afraid because he was naked. That day, Adam and Eve experienced something they had never experienced before. They were afraid. Sin brought fear. Like a flood, evil thoughts and attitudes filled their mind and heart. As the presence of God approached, they were terrified to reveal themselves to Him. Shame filled their hearts. This shame was because they had disobeyed. It was also because they were no longer the same and their relationship with God was affected. Now as they stood naked and exposed before God, all they could experience was the distance that now separated them. This brought deep shame and fear.

This fear was not just of God but also of each other. They covered themselves and distanced themselves from each other. Innocence was gone. They were ashamed of what they had become. They were ashamed of their thoughts, attitudes and intentions. They did whatever they could to hide this from God and from each other.

I suppose we have become so accustomed to our sinful thoughts and desires that we have a hard time understanding true innocence and integrity. Only in heaven will we understand the freedom from sin and its effect on our relationships with each other. We can only imagine at present what it will be like to serve and relate to God and to our brothers and sisters when sin no longer stands between us. Suffice it to say that sin devastated the pure and holy relationship between husband and wife.

Evidence of the effects of sin is seen not only in how they feared each other and covered themselves but also in how they responded to each other. When God asked them how they knew they were naked, Adam responded:

> *12 The man said, "The woman whom you gave to be with me, she gave me fruit of the tree, and I ate."*

Adam does not take personal responsibility for what happened that day. He blames God for giving him this broken woman and he blames his wife for deceiving him. Eve, on her part, blames Satan for deceiving her (see Genesis 3:13). No one takes the blame. No one confesses their sin or repents. Instead, they justify their actions and cast blame on each other. In this we see how sin caused them to become self-centred and self-preserving. There is no recognition of sin. There is no seeking forgiveness from God or each other. There are only excuses and an attempt to deflect blame.

Notice the punishment of God for this sin. God told Adam and Eve that they would experience pain in their daily routines. The earth would no longer produce its crops without painful toil on Adam's part. Eve would bear children in pain. The lives of these couple would become difficult and they would have to make their living by hard work. Their relationship would be strained not only because of sin in their lives but also because of the curse of God on the land.

Of significance to us is what God told Eve in Genesis 3:16 about her relationship with her husband:

16 To the woman he said,
"I will surely multiply your pain in childbearing;
in pain you shall bring forth children.
Your desire shall be contrary to your husband,
but he shall rule over you." (Genesis 3)

Notice the phrase "your desire shall be contrary to your husband, but he shall rule over you." This phrase is translated differently in the various versions of the Bible:

The King James version of the Bible translates:

"And thy desire shall be to thy husband,
And he shall rule over thee." (Genesis 3:16, KJV)

Notice that the words "shall be" are in italic to indicate that these words are not in the original Hebrew but are required to make sense in the English translation. The New King James and the New International

Version translates this in the same way with the words "shall be" in italics. This means then that the original text reads "your desire to/for your husband".

The New Living Translation reads as follows:

"And through your desire will be for your husband, he will be your master" (Genesis 3:16)

This translation adds a note to the verse for an alternative reading:

"And though you may desire to control your husband, he will be your master." (Genesis 3:16, NLT)

What is Genesis 3:16 saying? The answer seems to lie in our understanding of the word "desire" in this context. The Hebrew word for desire is *"teshuqah"*. It occurs only three times in the Old Testament. The AMG Word Study Dictionary defines this word as follows:

A feminine noun meaning longing. It is used to describe strong feelings of desire that one person had for another, but it was not always healthy desire. (Baker, Warren; Carpenter, Eugene, "8669 tesugah" AMG Word Study Dictionary, Cedar Rapids: Laridian)

What is important for us to note here is that the desire that this word describes is not always a healthy desire. This word only occurs two other times in the Old Testament. In Song of Solomon 7:10 we read:

*10 I am my beloved's,
and his desire is for me. (Song of Solomon 7)*

In this context the desire spoken of is of a positive nature. Her beloved longed for her and desired to be with her expressing his tender affections toward her.

The only other use of the word *"teshugah"* is found in Genesis 4:7:

7 If you do well, will you not be accepted? And if you do not do well, sin is crouching at the door. Its desire is contrary to you, but you must rule over it." (Genesis 7)

Here God is speaking to Cain who was experiencing tremendous jealousy and anger over the fact that God had rejected his offering while accepting the offering of his brother. God warned Cain that sin was at his door with its desire was for him. The desire of this sin was to make him fall. In fact, Cain gave into the desire of sin and killed his brother despite the warning of God.

In the context of Genesis 3 and the entrance of sin into the world, God tells Eve that she would have a desire toward her husband. This desire would not be a perfect desire. It would be stained by the sin that she was now experiencing in her life.

God also told Eve that day that her husband would rule over her. Remember again the context. In as much as Eve's desire would be tarnished by sin so would Adam's rule over his wife. Desire and authority have been tarnished by sin and now enters their relationship. They now compete for control. The loss of innocence and the entrance of self-centredness and pride had a devastating effect on the relationship of this couple. Their broken relationship with God crushed the union they once had.

This sin would become the source of many problem and temptations for the lives of this couple and all who would follow them. With the entrance of sin into the world, Satan did his utmost to pervert God's intention for the union of this first couple. If we are to understand God's intention for sexuality, we must also understand that we are living in a world that has fallen into sin. God's purpose has been perverted by sin and Satan. If we are to experience the unity that God intended, we must first deal with the sin that now stand between us.

For Consideration:

What was the effect of sin on the mind and heart of Adam and Eve?

Why did Adam and Eve need to cover themselves when sin entered the world? What does this tell us about the effect of sin on their lives and their relationship?

Consider the effect of sin on your relationship with your husband or wife. How does sin keep you from experiencing what God has intended for you?

For Prayer:

Take a moment to ask the Lord to reveal any sin in your relationship that makes you hid yourself or withdraw yourself from your partner.

Thank the Lord that while sin does come between us as husbands and wives, there is victory in the Lord Jesus?

Ask the Lord to help you to deal with the sin that would keep you from God and from experiencing what God intended with your partner in marriage.

3 - ONE FLESH

When sin entered the world, the relationship between God and His creation was tarnished. Sin also had a profound affect on the relationship between man and his wife. In this chapter I would like to return to a statement made by Adam in Genesis 2:24 about marriage and the intentions of God for a Biblical marriage:

24 Therefore a man shall leave his father and mother and hold fast to his wife, and they shall become one flesh. (Genesis 2)

These words were spoken by Adam when God presented him with his wife. They are prophetic in nature and speak about the purpose of God for a husband and wife. There are three details I want to examine in this passage.

Notice first, that Adam tells us that a man would leave his father and mother. This leaving is more than moving out. The idea here is that he would leave his parent's home to establish his own. He would take on the responsibility of providing for his own needs and those of a new family. He would become the head of a new household with all the obligations that came with this new position.

Second, this husband would take a wife and hold fast to her. The Hebrew word used for "hold fast" carries with it the idea of joining or staying with his wife. There is deep commitment in this word. He would join with his wife for life. He would stick with her through the difficult times. He would never leave her but remain with her as a provider and care giver.

Finally, it is in this context of leaving parents and holding fast to each other that Adam tells us that this couple would become one flesh. The one flesh relationship would thrive only under these conditions. Both partners would have to leave their father and mother or any relationship that would come between them. They would make it their commitment to remain faithful to each other and hold fast to each other no matter what happened.

This union between a man and his wife is blessed by God. The prophet Malachi tells us:

15 Did he not make them one, with a portion of

the Spirit in their union (Malachi 2)

What Malachi is telling us is that the blessing of God is on the couple who leave all others and commit themselves to each other. For an agreement to become binding, it often needs an official seal or signature. This is what is happening here. God makes the agreement between the husband and the wife official by blessing the union with a "portion of the Spirit." The Spirit given to this couple not only blesses the union but also empowers it to be all that God has desired it to become. The Spirit of God gives wisdom and strength for the couple to live together as husband and wife under the blessing of God.

From this blessing onward, God recognizes the union of this couple. Mark 10:8 tells us:

> *8 and the two shall become one flesh. So they are no longer two but one flesh (Mark 10)*

In God's eyes, this couple has been joined to work and function as one. Every decision one partner made will affect the other. They will work together in the raising of a family. They will compliment each other and minister to each other's needs.

The apostle Paul makes an interesting statement in 1 Corinthians 7:

4 For the wife does not have authority over her own body, but the husband does. Likewise the husband does not have authority over his own body, but the wife does. (1 Corinthians 7)

In an age of rebellion against authority, this statement is hard to accept. What we need to understand, however, is that marriage is a surrender of husband and wife to each other. While the immediate context of 1 Corinthians 7 is that of a sexual relationship, the application of this principle goes much deeper than this. The apostle Paul went on to say:

32 I want you to be free from anxieties. The unmarried man is anxious about the things of the Lord, how to please the Lord. 33 But the married man is anxious about worldly things, how to please his wife, 34 and his interests are divided. And the unmarried or betrothed woman is anxious about the things of the Lord, how to be holy in body and spirit. But the married woman is anxious about worldly things, how to please her husband. (1 Corinthians 7)

Consider what Paul told the Corinthians in verse 33. The married man is anxious about how to please his wife. This means that he is aware that his wife has the right to expect that his efforts and concerns be for her. She has the right to expect that when she is in need, he will reach out to her in that need. His strength is at her disposal. His concern is for her. He will devote time to her. He will use his resources to provide for her. What is true for the husband is also true for the wife. She gives herself body, mind and heart to care for him in his need. God expected that when the man left his family and held fast to his wife, he would care for her with selfless devotion. Both would see the needs of their partner as being as important as their own needs. Writing to the Philippians the apostle Paul would say:

> *3 Do nothing from selfish ambition or conceit, but in humility count others more significant than yourselves. 4 Let each of you look not only to his own interests, but also to the interests of others. (Philippians 2)*

If this is Paul's expectation for believers in the church, how much more should this be true for those whom God has declared to be one flesh? The enemy to a one flesh relationship is self-centredness and independent pride. All too many marriages have failed at this point. Instead of giving ourselves to the needs of our partners, we expect them to serve our needs. The starting point should never be my rights and needs but my partner's. If your body is not your own, then you have an obligation to use is for the good and well-being of your partner.

Paul would explain this further in Ephesians 5 when is said:

> *28 In the same way husbands should love their wives as their own bodies. He who loves his wife loves himself. 29 For no one ever hated his own flesh, but nourishes and cherishes it, just as Christ does the church, 30 because we are members of his body. 31 "Therefore a man shall leave his father and mother and hold fast to his wife, and the two shall become one flesh." (Ephesians 5)*

Paul told the Ephesians that the husband should love the wife as his own body. Because they are one flesh before God, they need to live as such. If a husband loves his wife, he loves himself because she is part of him. How do we love ourselves? When we are hungry we find food to eat. When we are tired we lay down to rest. We care for our bodies and do whatever we can to meet their needs. The apostle is challenging men to care for their wives as they would care for their own bodies.

God intends that the husband and wife be one flesh. If we understand this truly we will not see ourselves as separate from our partner but as one with him or her. We will reach out to minister to their needs and care for them as we would care for ourselves.

There is a world of difference between selfishness and being one flesh. The selfish person is concerned only for themselves. In fact, he or she may use their relationship to advance their own cause or meet their personal needs and have no concern for their partner. Being one flesh, on the other hand, recognizes the need of my partner and actively seeks his or her well-being. Being one flesh means valuing one's partner. It understands that when my partner suffers, I suffer also. When my partner thrives, I am most happy. When my partner is in pain I am in pain and will do all I can to minister to that pain. Being one flesh means protecting and nurturing my partner for in doing so I am caring for myself as well.

Adam's prophetic words in Genesis 2:24 are the basis for human sexuality. It is in this content of oneness, mutual concern and commitment that this relationship is to flourish. It is an exclusive relationship between a husband and a wife who care for each other and commit themselves to minister to each not only in the context of a sexual relationship but also in every aspect of their lives together.

For Consideration:

What does Genesis 2:24 teach us about the purpose of God for marriage between a man and a woman.

Malachi 2:15 tells us that God placed a portion of His Spirit on the one-flesh relationship between a husband and wife. What does this teach us about God's view of this relationship?

What does Paul mean when he says that in a one-flesh relationship the partners do not have exclusive rights to their own bodies? What is the implication of this in the relationship of a married couple?

What is the difference between being one-flesh and being selfish and self-centred? How is selfishness an enemy to a one-flesh relationship?

How does a Biblical one-flesh relationship provide a safe environment for a sexual relationship and any children that might come from that relationship? How does it provide for the well-being of a couple in general?

For Prayer:

If you are married, ask the Lord to show you if you have truly left all others to hold fast to your partner? Ask God to show you if there is anything that stands between you as a couple.

Thank the Lord that He has placed His blessing on your marriage in the person of the Holy Spirit who comes to empower and enable you to live in a one-flesh relationship.

Ask the Spirit of God to have full control of your marriage and to teach you how to consider the needs of your partner as your own. Ask Him to open your eyes to the needs of your partner. Ask Him to give you wisdom and strength to minister to those needs.

Ask the Lord to break any independent spirit that would keep you from being one with your partner. Ask Him to help you to grow in His purpose for you to be one-flesh in all that you do.

4 - OLD TESTAMENT UNCLEANNESS AND SEXUAL RELATIONS

As we continue our examination of what the Bible teaches about sexuality we come across some verses in Leviticus that seem to be somewhat perplexing.

16 "If a man has an emission of semen, he shall bathe his whole body in water and be unclean until the evening. 17 And every garment and every skin on which the semen comes shall be washed with water and be unclean until the evening. 18 If a man lies with a woman and has an emission of semen, both of them shall bathe themselves in water and be unclean until the evening. (Leviticus 15)

From what we have seen so far, God gave Eve to Adam to be his wife. It was His intention that they multiply and fill the earth. A sexual relationship was the means He ordained for this to take place. God blessed the union of this first couple. From Malachi 2:15 we saw that God places a portion of His Spirit on the union of a husband and wife in marriage. It comes as a surprise to us, therefore, that we read in Leviticus 15:18 that by engaging in the sexual act, the husband and wife would become unclean before God.

The Law of Moses would go even further than this. Listen to the command of God to the priests of Moses' day:

3 Say to them, 'If any one of all your offspring throughout your generations approaches the holy things that the people of Israel dedicate to the Lord, while he has an uncleanness, that person shall be cut off from my presence: I am the Lord. 4 None of the offspring of Aaron who has a leprous disease or a discharge may eat of the holy things until he is clean. Whoever touches anything that is unclean through contact with the dead or a man who has had an emission of semen, 5 and whoever touches a swarming thing by which he may be made unclean or a person from whom he may take uncleanness, whatever his uncleanness may be — 6 the person who touches such a thing shall be unclean until the evening and shall not eat of the holy things unless he has bathed his body in water.

What is significant here for us to see is that according to verse 4 if a priest had an emission of semen, he was forbidden to approach the holy things of God. He was unclean and could not perform his duties. If he disregarded this command of God, he was to be cut off from the presence of the Lord. Instead, he was to bath himself and remain unclean until the evening. Only then could he return to his duties.

1 Samuel 21 tells the story of how David was forced to flee from King Saul who sought to kill him. Because he had to leave in haste, he did not have time to pack for his journey. Arriving in the town of Nob, David went to see Ahimelech the priest. He asked the priest for food for him and his men. Ahimelech did not have anything to offer him but the holy bread that was on the table before the Lord. Listen to the account of this incident in 1 Samuel 21:4-6:

4 And the priest answered David, "I have no common bread on hand, but there is holy bread

—if the young men have kept themselves from women." 5 And David answered the priest, "Truly women have been kept from us as always when I go on an expedition. The vessels of the young men are holy even when it is an ordinary journey. How much more today will their vessels be holy?" 6 So the priest gave him the holy bread, for there was no bread there but the bread of the Presence, which is removed from before the Lord, to be replaced by hot bread on the day it is taken away.

Notice what is happening in this story. Ahimelech understood the Law of Moses that stated that no priest who had an emission of semen was permitted to touch the holy things of God. Out of compassion for David and his men, the priest was willing to offer this bread to them on one condition –they had to guarantee that none of them had had a sexual relationship with a woman that day. Only after being assured that none of these men were unclean through sexual activity, did the priest surrender this bread.

What is equally as significant in this passage is the response of David to the priest in verse 5. When asked if the men had engaged in any sexual activity that day, David responded:

5 ... "Truly women have been kept from us as always when I go on an expedition. The vessels of the young men are holy even when it is an ordinary journey. How much more today will their vessels be holy?" (1 Samuel 21)

David tells us that women were kept from the army on every expedition they undertook. In other words, David's men would not make themselves unclean through sexual activity when they were engaging in war against the enemy. The idea here is that they were to remain clean before the Lord when they went to battle.

This practice is confirmed in Deuteronomy 23 where we read:

> *9 "When you are encamped against your enemies, then you shall keep yourself from every evil thing. 10 "If any man among you becomes unclean because of a nocturnal emission, then he shall go outside the camp. He shall not come inside the camp, 11 but when evening comes, he shall bathe himself in water, and as the sun sets, he may come inside the camp. (Deuteronomy 23)*

If a soldier had an emission of semen while he slept, he was to leave the camp, bathe himself, and only return in the evening. The idea here is that this emission of semen would make him unclean and his presence in the camp could hinder the blessing of God on the army.

In Exodus 19 we read how the Lord descended on Mount Sinai in the presence of the people of Israel. To prepare the people for this presence, Moses consecrated the people. Listen to the words of Exodus 19:14-15:

> *14 So Moses went down from the mountain to the people and consecrated the people; and they washed their garments. 15 And he said to the people, "Be ready for the third day; do not go near a woman." (Exodus 19)*

The command of Moses was very clear. The Lord is going to descend on this mountain in three days. Because the Lord was going to make His presence known in their midst, they were not to engage in any sexual activity, making themselves unclean before Him.

While not as clear, the words of Joel seem to convey this same principle. Calling for a confession of sin and a fast of repentance the prophet says:

> *15 Blow the trumpet in Zion;*
> *consecrate a fast;*
> *call a solemn assembly;*
> *16 gather the people.*

Consecrate the congregation;
assemble the elders;
gather the children,
even nursing infants.
Let the bridegroom leave his room,
and the bride her chamber. (Joel 2)

According to Joel 2:16 the people were to be consecrated. One of the requirements of this consecration was that "the bridegroom was to leave his room, and the bride her chamber." In other words, they were to cease their sexual activity for this period of fasting. They were not to make themselves unclean by having a sexual relationship with their husband or wife during this time of seeking God's forgiveness and pardon.

Even in the New Testament we have a hint of this practice of abstaining from sexual activity while seeking the Lord in prayer and fasting. Listen to Paul's advice to the Corinthians in 1 Corinthians 7:5:

5 Do not deprive one another, except perhaps by agreement for a limited time, that you may devote yourselves to prayer; but then come together again, so that Satan may not tempt you because of your lack of self-control.

We will examine this passage in another context

later in this study. What we need to see, however, is that Paul told that Corinthians that it was acceptable, when there was an agreement between partners, to abstain from sexual activity when they were in a period of seeking God in prayer.

Leviticus 15:23 tells us that another means by which a man could become impure was by having a sexual relationship with his wife during her monthly period.

> *24 And if any man lies with her and her menstrual impurity comes upon him, he shall be unclean seven days, and every bed on which he lies shall be unclean. (Leviticus 15)*

In this case, the man was to be unclean for a period of seven days and anything he touched during that seven-day period became unclean.

What do we see here in these laws of the Old Testament? While God created human beings with a desire for sex and the population of the earth depended on this, the very act He created would make the couple who engaged in it unclean. Priests were not to perform their duties on the day that they had a sexual relationship with their wives. Soldiers fighting the enemy would not have sexual relations lest their uncleanness affected the outcome of the battle.

How are we to understand these laws of God and what does this teach us about the sexual relationship between a husband and wife? Let me conclude this chapter with a few words on this topic.

Uncleanness Versus Sin

The first point we need to make here is that there is a difference between uncleanness and sin. It is of significance that to be purified of the uncleanness caused by an emission of semen, all the husband and wife had to do was to bathe in water. There was no sacrifice required for this uncleanness. This is to say that the couple had not sinned by engaging in this sexual activity –they were simply unclean.

There were many other activities that would render an object or person unclean. A woman's menstrual period would make her unclean according to the Law of Moses (Leviticus 15:19-24). Touching a dead body required a period of seven days of purification (Numbers 19:16). When a family member died, someone had to take care of the body and see that it was properly disposed of. This required that the person involved become unclean for a period of time. This compassionate act of caring for a loved one was necessary, and God expected nothing less of His people. While it made the person unclean, it was required by God and not a sinful act.

While a sexual act between a husband and wife was blessed by God, He did require that the couple recognize that the emission of semen was an uncleanness that needed to be cleansed by water.

Health And Hygiene

Another issue of concern in the law of God was that of the health of the greater community. Anything that could cause the spread of disease was carefully monitored. In our day we understand that sexually transmitted diseases can be spread through bodily fluids. God has a concern for the health of His people. By requiring that the couple bathe and remain unclean until the evening, the Lord was protecting the entire community from disease and sickness. Sexual activity was not the only concern. Whole chapters of the Bible are devoted to skin diseases and mold in homes. All these things were to be monitored so that the community would not be infected with any kind of sickness.

Reminder Of The Holiness And Purity Of God

Finally, this period of uncleanness was a reminder to the couple of the absolute purity and holiness of God. Even the smallest defilement was an offence to Him. It was also, however, a reminder of the grace of God in accepting them even though they were unclean in many ways.

The fact of the matter is that we cannot live in

this world without becoming unclean. Our thoughts, our attitudes, our actions all make us unclean. The things we see around us or the things we hear from co-workers splatter us with uncleanness. Sin is everywhere-present. Our minds are filled daily with sinful images, words and thoughts. Those who are serious about their relationship with God will constantly seek cleansing from these daily defilements.

As we continue our examination of Biblical sexuality, we will see that while the sex act itself did make the couple unclean for a time, it was encouraged by God who blessed it for the good of the couple.

For Consideration:

What was the requirement of the Old Testament law for a married couple who had a sexual relationship? How could they become clean again?

How did having a sexual relationship with his wife affect what the priest could or could not do in the tabernacle or temple?

What was expected of soldiers who were engaged in battle?

What is the difference between becoming unclean

and sinning? Was it acceptable, given the right circumstances to become unclean. Was becoming unclean a sin?

How did the Law of Moses protect the health of the community of God's people?

What kind of things can make us unclean before God today?

For Prayer:

Ask the Lord to give you grace to understand the difference between being unclean and sinning.

Ask God to cleanse you of the defilements of this day so that these defilements will not hinder your relationship with Him.

Thank the Lord that while we are daily rendered unclean by living in this world, we can know the cleansing of the Lord.

5 - LEVIRATE MARRIAGES AND POLYGAMY

As we continue our study of God's purpose for human sexuality it is important that we examine a couple of practices found in the Old Testament. The first of these two practices is a marriage known as the levirate marriage.

Levirate Marriages

A levirate marriage took place when a husband died without giving his wife a child. If this was the case, the nearest male relative of the deceased husband was to take his widow as wife. The first child born to this union would be heir to the deceased husband's property and wealth.

5 "If brothers dwell together, and one of them dies and has no son, the wife of the dead man shall not be married outside the family to a stranger. Her husband's brother shall go in to her and take her as his wife and perform the duty of a husband's brother to her. 6 And the first son whom she bears shall succeed to the name of his dead brother, that his name may not be blotted out of Israel. (Deuteronomy 25)

This was the command of God for a wife who did not have a child when her husband died. The practice guaranteed that a widow of child bearing age was provided for and that the name of her first husband was not "blotted out of Israel" (Deuteronomy 25:6). To refuse to marry the wife of a deceased brother was to dishonour his widow and the name of the deceased. In fact, Deuteronomy 25:7-10 describes what would happen to the male descendant who refused to take on this responsibility:

7 And if the man does not wish to take his brother's wife, then his brother's wife shall go up to the gate to the elders and say, 'My husband's brother refuses to perpetuate his brother's name in Israel; he will not perform the duty of a husband's brother to me.' 8 Then the elders of his city shall call him and speak to him, and if he persists, saying, 'I do not wish to take her,' 9 then his brother's wife shall go up to him in the presence of the elders and pull his sandal off his foot and spit in his face. And she shall answer and say, 'So shall it be done to the man who does not build up his brother's house.' 10 And the name of his house shall be called in Israel, 'The house of him who had his sandal pulled off.' (Deuteronomy 25)

Four things took place when a man refused to marry his brother's widow and provide for her need. First, she would report the matter to the elders of the city. Second, these elders would meet with the man to convince him to take on his responsibility. Third, if he refused even after meeting with the elders, the widow was to approach him, pull of his sandal and spit in his face. This was in response to the insult and dishonour the man had expressed to her and his brother. Finally, the household of this man would from that point on bear the shame of their unwillingness to help. His household would be known in the community as "the house of him who had his sandal pulled off" (Deuteronomy 25:10).

We have a couple of examples of this practice of levirate marriage in the Old Testament. The first example of this is found in Genesis 38:6-10. Judah had three sons, Er, Onan and Shelah. His first son Er married a woman by the name of Tamar. Because

Er was an evil man, the Lord struck him so that he died without giving his wife Tamar a child. Notice the response of Judah when this happened:

> *8 Then Judah said to Onan, "Go in to your brother's wife and perform the duty of a brother-in-law to her, and raise up offspring for your brother." (Genesis 38)*

It was expected that Onan have a sexual relationship with his brother's wife and provide her with a child. Onan, however, knew that the child born to this relationship would not be his. Notice what he did in Genesis 38:9:

> *9 But Onan knew that the offspring would not be his. So whenever he went in to his brother's wife he would waste the semen on the ground, so as not to give offspring to his brother. (Genesis 38)*

Onan had a sexual relationship with his brother's wife, but he refused to impregnate her, choosing to spill his semen on the ground instead. The Lord became so angry with Onan over this that He struck him dead (see Genesis 38:10). By refusing to provide an offspring for his brother through Tamar, Onan disobeyed the law of God and brought about his own judgement.

Another example of a levirate marriage is found in the book of Ruth. Ruth was a widow whose husband had died without giving her a child. The brother of Ruth's deceased husband also died. As a widow, Ruth settled in the region of Bethlehem with her mother-in-law, Naomi. There in the region of Bethlehem was a male relative by the name of Boaz. When Naomi discovered that Boaz was in the region, she immediately set in motion a plan to have him marry Ruth and provide her with a child to continue her family name.

The opportunity came for Ruth to ask Boaz to be a redeemer for her so that the name of her husband would not be blotted out. Listen to the response of Boaz to this request:

> *12 And now it is true that I am a redeemer. Yet there is a redeemer nearer than I. 13 Remain tonight, and in the morning, if he will redeem you, good; let him do it. But if he is not willing to redeem you, then, as the Lord lives, I will redeem you. (Ruth 3)*

While Boaz was quite willing to marry Ruth and provide her with a child to carry on her deceased husband's name, he was aware that this responsibility, according to law, was to go to the nearest male relative. There was a closer relative who had this obligation.

Boaz went before the elders of the city and called this relative to his side. He offered him the opportunity to redeem a parcel of land and to take Ruth as his wife.

> *5 Then Boaz said, "The day you buy the field from the hand of Naomi, you also acquire Ruth the Moabite, the widow of the dead, in order to perpetuate the name of the dead in his inheritance." (Ruth 4)*

Hearing that he would have to marry Ruth and provide her with a child to inherit the property of her first husband, the relative refused the offer, turning the obligation over to Boaz as the next of kin. This matter was sealed by the removal of a sandal (Ruth 4:7). The result of this marriage between Boaz and Ruth was a child by the name of Obed who would carry on the name of Ruth's first husband.

The levirate marriage was designed to provide for a childless widow. It was the obligation of the closest male relative to care for her and give her a child to carry on her first husband's name. It assured that his property was not lost to the family and that his widow would be provided for after his death.

The New Testament does not impose this law on widows. Instead, the apostle Paul encouraged widows to remain single (1 Corinthians 7:8-9). He also called on the church to care for widows who had no family to care for them (1 Timothy 5:9-16).

Polygamy

The second practice found in the Old Testament is polygamy. Polygamy is the practice of taking more than one wife. There are numerous cases of men who had more than one wife in the Old Testament. The most notable of these was Solomon. 1 Kings 11:3 tells us that he had 700 wives and 300 concubines. While there is reference to polygamous marriages in the Scripture this was not the common practice of the day. The Tyndale Bible Commentary has this to say about polygamy:

> *Despite numerous examples of polygamy cited in the OT, there is no doubt that the vast majority of the Israelites were monogamous. There are no examples given of large polygamous marriages in the families of commoners. (Comfort, Philip W., Elwell, Walter A., "Marriage, Marriage Customs," Tyndale Bible Dictionary: Cedar Rapids: Laridian, 2001)*

Most of the Jewish marriages in the Old Testament were between one husband and one wife. When God presented Adam his wife, Adam declared:

> *[24] Therefore a man shall leave his father and*

his mother and hold fast to his wife, and they
shall become one flesh. (Genesis 2)

Notice that the word "wife" is singular. The idea is that it was God's intention that a man take only one wife. The use of the word "wife" in the singular is repeated often in the Old Testament laws (see Exodus 20:17, Exodus 21:5, Leviticus 18:8, Leviticus 20:10). Again, this expresses the purpose of God for a marriage between one man and one woman.

While polygamy was not God's intention for His people, they did not always walk in His purpose. Even godly men chose to take more than one wife. Those who did take more than one wife, however, were obligated to care for them and provide all their needs.

[10] If he takes another wife to himself, he shall not diminish her food, her clothing, or her marital rights. [11] And if he does not do these three things for her, she shall go out for nothing, without payment of money. (Exodus 21)

Notice particularly that the man who took a second wife was obliged to provide her with food, clothing and marital rights. Verse 10 tells us that he was not to "diminish" any of these necessities. In other words, he was to provide her with all she required. She was not to be in need. Of interest to us here is the reference to "marital rights." The Hebrew word used here is the word "ônāh". The AMG Complete Word Study Dictionary defines this word in the following way:

> *A feminine noun referring to conjugal rights, the duty of marriage. It refers to the right of a wife in a polygamous marriage to have intimacy with her husband (Ex 21:10). (Baker, Warren; Carpenter, Eugene, "5772 ônāh" AMG Complete Word Study Bible, Cedar Rapids: Laridian, 2003)*

The Law of Moses required that a man have sexual relations with his wife and if he took a second wife this was not to diminish. Each wife had the right to a sexual relationship with her husband.

Deuteronomy 21 makes it quite clear that a man was not to show favouritism when it came to the children born to these wives.

> *[15] "If a man has two wives, the one loved and the other unloved, and both the loved and the unloved have borne him children, and if the firstborn son belongs to the unloved, [16] then on the day when he assigns his possessions as an inheritance to his sons, he may not treat the son of the loved as the firstborn in preference to the son of the unloved, who is the firstborn, [17] but he shall acknowledge the firstborn, the son*

*of the unloved, by giving him a double portion
of all that he has, for he is the firstfruits of
his strength. The right of the firstborn is his.
(Deuteronomy 21)*

This passage shows us one of the reasons for polygamy in those days. Sometimes the man and woman in the marriage ceased to love each other. It may be that there was no legitimate reason for divorce. Maybe, out of respect for her or for a desire to keep his reputation, the husband may have chosen to provide for his unloved wife. He may have chosen another wife to meet the emotional needs she was not meeting. For whatever reason the man may have taken another wife, the Old Testament required that the firstborn son of that first relationship was to inherit the father's estate. His obligations to this son of the unloved wife were not to change. Before God the legitimate heir was the son of his first wife.

The practice of polygamy was discouraged in the New Testament. If a man wanted to be a leader in the church, he needed to be the husband of only one wife.

*[2] Therefore an overseer must be above
reproach, the husband of one wife, sober-
minded, self-controlled, respectable, hospitable,
able to teach (1 Timothy 3)*

[5] This is why I left you in Crete, so that you might put what remained into order, and appoint elders in every town as I directed you — [6] if anyone is above reproach, the husband of one wife, and his children are believers and not open to the charge of debauchery or insubordination. (Titus 1)

[12] Let deacons each be the husband of one wife, managing their children and their own households well. (1 Timothy 3)

While polygamy was practiced by some individuals in the Old Testament, it was not the intention of God from the beginning. If a man did take another wife, however, he was obligated to care for her and give her all the attention he gave to his other wives. In New Testament times, those who did take more than one wife, were not permitted to function as leader in the church.

For Consideration:

What is the practice of levirate marriage in the Old Testament? What is our obligation as a church today toward widows?

Was it God's intention that a man have more than one wife? Does the practice of polygamy in the Old Testament mean that God intended that man have more than one wife?

God's law imposed clear obligations on those who did take more than one wife. What is the difference between protecting women in a polygamous relationship and condoning the practice?

What does the New Testament teach about church leaders and polygamy?

For Prayer:

Are there widows in your community that need support and encouragement? Ask the Lord to show you how you can minister to them as a church in their time of need.

If you are married, ask the Lord to develop your love toward your husband or wife. Ask Him to help you to be faithful to them and to minister fully to all their needs.

6 - CONCUBINES AND SURROGATE RELATIONSHIPS

In the last chapter we examined the levirate marriages and polygamy as found in the Old Testament. Closely related to this was the practice of taking concubines. Easton's Bible Dictionary defines a concubine as follows:

Concubine in the Bible denotes a female conjugally united to a man but in a relationship inferior to that of a wife...The concubine was a wife of secondary rank. (Easton, M.G., "Concubine", Easton's Bible Dictionary, Cedar Rapids: Laridian).

The concubine was not a prostitute. She was dedicated to the man with whom she had a sexual relation and was provided for on a regular basis by this man. It was considered shameful for a concubine to have a sexual relationship with any other man. This is seen clearly in Genesis 35 when Reuben was found guilty of sleeping with his father's concubine.

> *[22] While Israel lived in that land, Reuben went and lay with Bilhah his father's concubine. And Israel heard of it. (Genesis 35)*

In Genesis 49 Jacob, Reuben's father speaks to all his sons and pronounces his blessings on them. Listen to the words he had to say to Reuben:

> *[3] "Reuben, you are my firstborn,*
> *my might, and the firstfruits of my strength,*
> *preeminent in dignity and preeminent in power.*
> *[4] Unstable as water, you shall not have pre-*
> *eminence,*
> *because you went up to your father's bed;*
> *then you defiled it—he went up to my couch!*
> *(Genesis 49)*

While Reuben was the firstborn of Jacob, and the one who was to receive the greatest inheritance, Jacob called him unstable and to told him that he would not enjoy the privileges his position as first born offered. The reason for this was because he had defiled his father's bed by sleeping with his concubine. This was a tremendous insult to Jacob and one for which Reuben would pay heavily. 1 Chronicles tells us what would happen to Reuben.

> *[5:1] The sons of Reuben the firstborn of Israel (for he was the firstborn, but because he defiled his father's couch, his birthright was given to the sons of Joseph the son of Israel, so that he could not be enrolled as the oldest son; (1 Chronicles 5)*

Reuben was disinherited. He was not given his birthright because he had slept with his father's concubine.

Another detail to notice is that the children born to a concubine did not have the status of those born to a wife. Abraham had children though concubines but only one son by his wife Sarah. Notice what Genesis 25 tells us about the inheritance of these children:

> *[5] Abraham gave all he had to Isaac. [6] But to the sons of his concubines Abraham gave gifts, and while he was still living he sent them away from his son Isaac, eastward to the east country. (Genesis 25)*

Abraham's sons, born to his concubines, did not receive an inheritance. While Isaac was given all that Abram had, these other sons were given gifts and sent away. God's purpose would be worked out through Isaac, the son of his true wife.

There is a record of Old Testament men taking concubines. Solomon had three hundred concubines (1 Kings 11:3). We also have records of Gideon (Judges 8:29-30) and Saul (2 Samuel 3:7) both of which took concubines.

It is important to note that this practice was not approved by Scripture. The fact that these men of God took concubines does not make their actions right. The New Testament is quite clear that when a married man has a sexual relationship with a woman who is not his wife, he is committing adultery. We will examine this in greater detail at a later point in this study.

Surrogate Mothers

Another practice found in the book of Genesis was that of a wife having children through her maid. The first occurrence of this is found in Genesis 16.

> *1 Now Sarai, Abram's wife, had borne him no children. She had a female Egyptian servant whose name was Hagar. 2 And Sarai said to*

Abram, "Behold now, the Lord has prevented me from bearing children. Go in to my servant; it may be that I shall obtain children by her." And Abram listened to the voice of Sarai. 3 So, after Abram had lived ten years in the land of Canaan, Sarai, Abram's wife, took Hagar the Egyptian, her servant, and gave her to Abram her husband as a wife. (Genesis 16)

Notice what is happening here. Sarah was not able to have children, so she told her husband to sleep with Hagar and have children through her. What is of significance for us to note are the words of Sarah in verse 2: "that I may obtain children by her." In other words, the children born to this sexual union of Abraham and Sarah's servant would be Sarah's children and not Hagar's. Hagar would bear children for Sarah, who was unable to get pregnant.

We see another occurrence of this practice in Genesis 30:

1 When Rachel saw that she bore Jacob no children, she envied her sister. She said to Jacob, "Give me children, or I shall die!" 2 Jacob's anger was kindled against Rachel, and he said, "Am I in the place of God, who has withheld from you the fruit of the womb?" 3 Then she said, "Here is my servant Bilhah; go in to her, so that she may give birth on my behalf, that even I may have children through her." 4 So she gave him her servant Bilhah as a wife, and Jacob went in to her. 5 And Bilhah conceived and bore Jacob a son. 6 Then Rachel said, "God has judged me, and has also heard my voice and given me a son." Therefore she called his name Dan. (Genesis 30)

Again, notice several details in this passage. When Rachel could not get pregnant, she gave Jacob her servant to bear children for her. Rachel's understanding was that her servant Bilhah would give birth on her behalf and that she would have children through her (verse 3). When a son was born through this sexual union of Jacob and Bilhah, Rachel said: God has judged me, and has also heard my voice and given me a son (verse 4). There was no doubt in the mind of Rachel that this child belonged to her and not to her servant who was only acting on her behalf.

Jacob' second wife Leah, seeing that she has stopped bearing children gave Jacob her servant Zilpah to bear children on her behalf (see Genesis 30:9). Out of the twelve sons of Jacob, four of them were born to him through Zilpah and Bilhah, the servants of his two wives.

It is of importance to note here that that there was a difference between the offspring of the concubine and that of a surrogate mother who bore children on behalf of her master. The children of the concubine did not inherit the property of their father. The father's inheritance was given to the children of his wife.

This is not the case for the child born to a surrogate mother. This child belonged to the wife and would be considered her child even though he or she was born to another mother. Dan, Naphtali, Asher and Gad, born to Bilhah and Zilpah, were given equal status with their brothers.

The only references to the practice of surrogate mothers bearing children for a barren wife are found in the book of Genesis. The practice was not without its problems. In the case of Sarah and her servant Hagar, there was bitter jealousy between the two women. Sarah began to mistreat her servant after she bore a child to Abraham. Hagar would run away from Sarah to escape the abuse (see Genesis 16).

It was the intense desire of Sarah, Rachel and Leah to have children and when they couldn't, they resorted to giving their servants to their husbands. What is of significance for us to note here, however, is that each of these women would eventually bear their own children as God opened their womb in His time. This leaves us to understand that these women were not acting from God so much as they were out of a sense of desperation. They took matters into their own hands.

As we move into the New Testament, the practice of having a child with a woman who is not one's wife would be considered adultery. Couples that are not able to have children have other options in our day.

There have been those who justify their sexual activities on the basis that the saints of the Old Testament practiced polygamy, had concubines or bore children through their servants. This argument is not legitimate. David committed adultery with another man's wife, but this does not prove that the practice was acceptable. He had a high price to pay for his sin. From the beginning of time, men and women have wandered from the purpose of God for their sexual lives. We have examples of this throughout the Scriptures.

The Law of Moses does regulate the practice of polygamy. This, however, was to protect the women who were in this kind of marriage, not to encourage its practice. Built into the Law of Moses were principles that were intended to protect the vulnerable from abuse. For example, in the Gospel of Matthew, the Pharisees came to Jesus to speak to Him about the question of divorce. In Matthew 19 they asked Jesus if a man could divorce his wife for any reason. Jesus told them that it was the purpose of God that a man and a woman be joined together as one flesh for life (see Matthew 19: 3-6). The Pharisees then asked Jesus why Moses made provision for divorce if it was not the will of God that a man divorce his wife:

7 They said to him, "Why then did Moses

command one to give a certificate of divorce and to send her away?" 8 He said to them, "Because of your hardness of heart Moses allowed you to divorce your wives, but from the beginning it was not so. 9 And I say to you: whoever divorces his wife, except for sexual immorality, and marries another, commits adultery." (Matthew 19)

The Pharisees bring up a very important point here. If it were not the purpose of God that a man divorces his wife, why did Moses allow it in the law? Jesus answers this by telling the Pharisees that the reason Moses made a law that was contrary to the purpose of God for a couple was because of the hardness of human hearts. In other words, there were times when a wife was being so abused by her husband that the merciful thing to do was to set her free from her obligations toward him. While divorce was not the will of God, there were times when it was better, according to the Law of Moses, to divorce one's husband than to be abused and harm the children in that union. The Law of Moses does not encourage divorce but provides a solution for extreme situations where remaining in a marriage would be destructive. The Lord is compassionate and merciful, and this is evident in the Law of Moses.

Why is it important that we understand what Jesus is teaching in this context? The fact that the Law of

God permits something, does not mean that it is His perfect will. The law regulated polygamy not because it was God's will but because God knew that there would be many who practiced polygamy, contrary to His purpose, and He wanted to provide protection for those who might be abused in this relationship.

The taking of concubines, polygamy and other such relationships were not the original purpose of God for humankind. He had a better standard for them. A man would leave his father and mother and become one flesh with his wife. They would live together as one before Him for the rest of their lives. They would turn from all others and minister to one another as God intended. Through this husband and wife, the world would be populated, and a new generation born to walk in the purpose of God.

For Consideration:

What was the difference between a concubine and a prostitute?

How were the children of a concubine treated differently from those of the true wife?

How does the New Testament view the practice of taking a concubine?

Do you think that Sarah, Rachel and Leah were right to give their servants to their husbands to have children through them? What does the fact that God gave all of them children of their own show us?

What is the difference between regulating a practice and encouraging its practice?

Does the fact that an Old Testament saint practiced something make it right? How important is it for us to examine the teaching of all of Scripture and not just certain passages?

For Prayer:

Have you ever taken matters into your own hands because you did not have the patience to wait on the Lord? Ask the Lord to give you greater patience to wait on Him and His timing.

Ask the Lord to help you not to be sidetracked from the truth because someone you respect has gone astray.

Thank the Lord that He is merciful and compassionate and bears with us in our shortcomings and failures.

Ask the Lord for grace in the application of the law. Ask Him to forgive you for times when you have not been patient with fellow believers and have hurt them by the harsh and merciless application of the law.

7 - ADULTERY

We saw how God created marriage in Genesis 2 by giving the first man a wife and blessed that union so that they became "one flesh." Marriage creates a union between a man and a woman that is to be held in honour and never broken. Listen to the words of the writer to the Hebrews:

4 Let marriage be held in honor among all, let the marriage bed be undefiled, for God will judge the sexually immoral and adulterous. (Hebrews 13)

The verse is very clear. The sexual relationship between a husband and wife is an honourable one. It is not to be defiled by adultery. God expects faithfulness between a husband and a wife. In fact, according to Hebrews 13:4 God will judge those who break this relationship through sexual unfaithfulness.

Adultery refers to a sexual relationship with someone other than one's husband or wife. Jesus expanded this definition of adultery to include lusting after another person's husband or wife. We will look at this under another heading later in this study.

There can be not doubt that adultery is forbidden in the Bible. The first reference to this is included in the Ten Commandments as found in Exodus 20:14: "You shall not commit adultery" (see also Deuteronomy 5:18). The breaking of this commandment was so serious that the Law of Moses commanded that those guilty of this sin be put to death:

> *10 "If a man commits adultery with the wife of his neighbor, both the adulterer and the adulteress shall surely be put to death. (Leviticus 20)*

Deuteronomy 22:22 repeats the same command but reminds us why death was to be the punishment for adultery:

> *22 "If a man is found lying with the wife of another man, both of them shall die, the man who lay with the woman, and the woman. So you shall purge the evil from Israel. (Deuteronomy 22)*

The practice of adultery was so evil in the eyes of God that it needed to be purged from the land. Both the man and the women were to be killed for their sin. In this case, there was no sacrifice provided for the forgiveness of the sin of adultery.

The Lord describes the sin of adultery as being "outrageous" in Jeremiah 29:

> *23 because they have done an outrageous thing in Israel, they have committed adultery with their neighbors' wives, and they have spoken in my name lying words that I did not command them. I am the one who knows, and I am witness, declares the Lord.'" (Jeremiah 29)*

The Hebrew word used for "outrageous" is the word "nebelah" which is defined by the AMG Complete Word Study Dictionary as follows:

> *nebelah: A feminine noun meaning folly, a disgraceful act. It refers to deeds that are especially serious, grave, sinful arrogant ... (Baker, Warren; Carpenter, Eugene: AMG Word Study Dictionary of the Old Testament, "5039 nebalah" Cedar Rapids: Laridian)*

The use of this word by God through Jeremiah shows

us that in His mind adultery is a serious offense.

Probably some of the greatest warnings of Scripture about the sin of adultery are found in the book of Proverbs. In Proverbs 5 we have a warning given to a son by a father. The context of chapter 5 makes it quite clear that the son is married. The father encouraged his son to delight in his own wife and not to "embrace the bosom of an adulteress" (see Proverbs 5:15-20). The adulteress is described as a "forbidden woman" (Proverbs 5:3). Listen to the words of the father to his son about this forbidden woman:

1 My son, be attentive to my wisdom;
incline your ear to my understanding,
2 that you may keep discretion,
and your lips may guard knowledge.
3 For the lips of a forbidden woman drip honey,
and her speech is smoother than oil,
4 but in the end she is bitter as wormwood,
sharp as a two-edged sword.
5 Her feet go down to death;
her steps follow the path to Sheol (Proverbs 5)

The wise father tells his son that the temptation to commit adultery will be very real. The lips of the forbidden women will "drip honey." Her enticing speech would be smoother than oil. In the end, however, she was as bitter as wormwood. She would pierce him like a sharp sword and lead him straight to death and the grave.

Listen to the words of Proverbs 6 concerning the sin of adultery:

> *23 For the commandment is a lamp and the teaching a light,*
> *and the reproofs of discipline are the way of life,*
> *24 to preserve you from the evil woman,*
> *from the smooth tongue of the adulteress.*
> *25 Do not desire her beauty in your heart,*
> *and do not let her capture you with her eyelashes;*
> *26 for the price of a prostitute is only a loaf of bread,*
> *but a married woman hunts down a precious life.*
> *(Proverbs 6)*

The adulteress is described as a smoothed tongued, evil woman who enticed her prey. She is compared to a prostitute in verse 26. The prostitute will offer her services for a loaf of bread to feed her family. The adulterous woman, however, will cost your life. Those caught in adultery were to be killed according to the Law of Moses.

The writer of the Proverbs would go on to compare the adulteress to a destructive fire:

27 Can a man carry fire next to his chest
and his clothes not be burned?
28 Or can one walk on hot coals
and his feet not be scorched?
29 So is he who goes in to his neighbor's wife;
none who touches her will go unpunished.
(Proverbs 6)

The punishment of God will fall on all who commit adultery and violate the commitment they have made to their marriage partner. To commit adultery, according to the writer of the Proverb is to destroy oneself:

32 He who commits adultery lacks sense;
he who does it destroys himself (Proverbs 6)

Proverbs 7 describes a young man enticed by a married woman whose husband had gone on a long journey (Proverbs 7:19). She lures him to her bedroom and he surrenders to her. Listen to the description of what happened that day:

21 With much seductive speech she persuades him;
with her smooth talk she compels him.
22 All at once he follows her,

as an ox goes to the slaughter,
or as a stag is caught fast
23 till an arrow pierces its liver;
as a bird rushes into a snare;
he does not know that it will cost him his life.
(Proverbs 7)

The results of following the adulteress to her bed were devastating. The young man is described as an ox going to the slaughter and a bird or deer caught in a trap. An arrow pierced his liver that day and cost him his life.

Solomon goes on to warn the young men of his day about the adulteress:

24 And now, O sons, listen to me,
and be attentive to the words of my mouth.
25 Let not your heart turn aside to her ways;
do not stray into her paths,
26 for many a victim has she laid low,
and all her slain are a mighty throng.
27 Her house is the way to Sheol,
going down to the chambers of death. (Proverbs
7)

The adulteress has had many victims. Her house is described as the way to Sheol (hell and the grave) and her bedroom as the chamber of death.

The New Testament also sees the sin of adultery as a very serious sin. Writing to the Corinthians the apostle Paul said:

> *9 Or do you not know that the unrighteous will not inherit the kingdom of God? Do not be deceived: neither the sexually immoral, nor idolaters, nor adulterers, nor men who practice homosexuality, 10 nor thieves, nor the greedy, nor drunkards, nor revilers, nor swindlers will inherit the kingdom of God. (1 Corinthians 6)*

Adultery is listed among the many sins of those who will not inherit the kingdom of God.

Listen to what the Lord Jesus told his listeners in Matthew 15:

> *19 For out of the heart come evil thoughts, murder, adultery, sexual immorality, theft, false witness, slander. 20 These are what defile a person. But to eat with unwashed hands does not defile anyone."*

Adultery is listed by Jesus among the sins that defile a person.

Returning to the passage we began with at the beginning of this chapter we read:

4 Let marriage be held in honor among all, and let the marriage bed be undefiled, for God will judge the sexually immoral and adulterous. (Hebrews 13)

God will judge those who defile their vows of faithfulness toward a marriage partner.

There can be no doubt that God takes the sin of adultery seriously. There are many warnings in Scripture about the dangers of falling into this sin and the judgement of God on those who do. It was a sin in the Old Testament that was punishable by death. It is, however, a sin for which we do have forgiveness in the New Testament.

John 8 describes a scene when Jesus was teaching in the temple. The Pharisees brought to Him a woman who had been caught in the act of adultery. They reminded Jesus that the Law of Moses commanded that such a woman be stoned to death (John 8:5). They asked Jesus what He felt they should do. Jesus told them that the person who had no sin was to be the one to cast first stone to kill her. When no one was willing to admit that they were without sin, Jesus spoke to the woman:

10 Jesus stood up and said to her, "Woman, where are they? Has no one condemned you?"

11 She said, "No one, Lord." And Jesus said, "Neither do I condemn you; go, and from now on sin no more." (John 8)

In Jesus, there was forgiveness for this adulterous woman. Notice, however, that while Jesus told her that He did not condemn her to death, He did tell her that what she had done was sin when He commanded her: "from now on sin no more" (verse 11).

God values marriage and expects that those who are married will be sexually faithful to each other. This means rejecting all temptations to have a sexual relationship with anyone but one's husband or wife.

For Consideration:

What is adultery? What does this sin teach us about the importance of sexual faithfulness in marriage?

What was the Old Testament punishment for adultery? Is there forgiveness today for the sin of adultery?

What are some of the warnings in Proverbs 5-7 about the adulteress? Why is adultery seen in Proverbs as being such a serious sin?

Is adultery only a sin against one's marriage partner?

How is it also a sin against God? How does this sin also affect our families and society?

For Prayer:

Have you ever been sexually unfaithful to your marriage partner? Ask God to forgive you and help you to recover from the effects of this unfaithfulness? Ask Him to show you what the results of this unfaithfulness have been in your life, in the life of your partner and in your relationship with God.

Ask God to protect you and your sexual relationship with your husband or wife. Ask Him to give you a deeper understanding of His purpose.

Take a moment to pray for the couples in your church? Ask God to build them up and give them a deeper commitment to walk in His purpose for their marriage.

8 - PROSTITUTION

We will now consider the teaching of Scripture about the practice of prostitution. This usually refers to a sexual relationship with an individual, known or unknown, either for personal or religious gain. We have a record of several prostitutes in the Old Testament.

In Genesis 38 we have the story of a woman by the name of Tamar, the daughter-in-law of Judah. She had been married to two of Judah's sons and they both died without giving her a child. According to the levirate law, Judah's third son was to marry her and give her a child. Judah, however, hesitated to give this son to Tamar since his two older sons had died while she was their wife. Being childless, Tamar disguised herself as a prostitute and slept with Judah, her father-in-law.

Joshua 2 recounts the story of another prostitute by

the name of Rahab who protected the Israelite spies who had come into the region of Canaan to spy out the land. Judges 16:1 tells us that Samson slept with a prostitute. Jephthah, who would deliver Israel from the oppression of the Ammonites, was the son of a prostitute (see Judges 11:1).

In the Old Testament, three types of prostitutes are mentioned. The first was the prostitute who offered sexual services for personal gain. In the story of Tamar and Judah, as recorded in Genesis 38, when Judah approached Tamar (disguised as a prostitute) she asked him what he would give her to have sex with him:

[16] He turned to her at the roadside and said, "Come, let me come in to you," for he did not know that she was his daughter-in-law. She said, "What will you give me, that you may come in to me?" [17] He answered, "I will send you a young goat from the flock." And she said, "If you give me a pledge, until you send it—" (Genesis 38)

We read about the price of a prostitute in Proverbs 6:

[26] for the price of a prostitute is only a loaf of bread, but a married woman hunts down a precious life. (Proverbs 6)

The reference to a loaf of bread for the services of a prostitute shows us that in some cases, this was the only source of income for these prostitutes who may have had children to feed.

The second type of prostitute was a religious prostitute. In fact, when Judah slept with Tamar he thought she was a cult prostitute. He sent his servant to pay the price for her services. Listen to the words of Judah's servant in Genesis 38:21:

[21] And he asked the men of the place, "Where is the cult prostitute who was at Enaim at the roadside?" And they said, "No cult prostitute has been here."

Commenting on this second type of prostitute, the IVP Bible Background Commentary says:

The Canaanite culture utilized cult prostitution as a way of promoting fertility. Devotees of the mother goddess Ishtar or Anat would reside at or near shrines and would dress in a veil, as the symbolic bride of the god Baal or El. Men would visit the shrine and use the services of the cult prostitutes prior to planting their fields or during other important seasons such as shearing or the period of lambing. In this way they gave honor to the gods and reenacted the divine marriage in an attempt to insure fertility and prosperity for their fields and herds. (Walton, John H.; Matthews, Victor H.; Chavalas, Mark W., The IVP Bible Background Commentary, Old

Testament, Notes on Genesis 38:15-23, Cedar Rapids: Laridian, 2000)

These cult prostitutes were part of the established pagan religions. Men and women engaged in sexual relations as a means of guaranteeing a harvest. This became part of the ritualistic religious practices of the day.

The final type of prostitute described in the Old Testament were foreign women who enticed the men of Israel to turn from the one true God to serve the gods of the nations around them. This appeared to be a significant problem in Israel and one that is addressed numerous times. Solomon appears to be the greatest offender in this regard:

[11:1] Now King Solomon loved many foreign women, along with the daughter of Pharaoh: Moabite, Ammonite, Edomite, Sidonian, and Hittite women, [2] from the nations concerning which the LORD had said to the people of Israel, "You shall not enter into marriage with them, neither shall they with you, for surely they will turn away your heart after their gods." Solomon clung to these in love. [3] He had 700 wives, who were princesses, and 300 concubines. And his wives turned away his heart. [4] For when Solomon was old his wives turned away his heart after other gods, and his heart was not

wholly true to the LORD his God, as was the heart of David his father. (1 Kings 11)

Numbers 25 recounts the story of how the Moabite women enticed the men of Israel, by having sexual relations with them, to offer sacrifices to their pagan gods:

[25:1] While Israel lived in Shittim, the people began to whore with the daughters of Moab. [2] These invited the people to the sacrifices of their gods, and the people ate and bowed down to their gods. [3] So Israel yoked himself to Baal of Peor. And the anger of the LORD was kindled against Israel. (Numbers 25)

While there is ample evidence in both the Old and New Testament of the practice of prostitution, the Bible is abundantly clear about what God thinks about the practice. The Law of Moses strictly forbid any Israelite male or female to become a cult prostitute:

[17] "None of the daughters of Israel shall be a cult prostitute, and none of the sons of Israel shall be a cult prostitute. (Deuteronomy 23)

If a priest's daughter became a prostitute, she profaned the name of her father and his position and as such was to be burned to death:

[9] And the daughter of any priest, if she profanes herself by whoring, profanes her father; she shall be burned with fire. (Leviticus 21)

The Law of Moses described prostitution as a profanity. The land that allowed the practice of prostitution, according to the law of the Old Testament was full of depravity:

[29] "Do not profane your daughter by making her a prostitute, lest the land fall into prostitution and the land become full of depravity. (Leviticus 19)

In no case were the wages of a prostitute to be used in the work of the temple. These wages are described in Deuteronomy 23:18 as an abomination:

[18] You shall not bring the fee of a prostitute or the wages of a dog into the house of the LORD your God in payment for any vow, for both of these are an abomination to the LORD your God. (Deuteronomy 23)

Old Testament priests were not to marry a prostitute.

To do so would be to profane his office and his offspring:

> *[7] They shall not marry a prostitute or a woman who has been defiled, neither shall they marry a woman divorced from her husband, for the priest is holy to his God. (Leviticus 21)*

> *[14] A widow, or a divorced woman, or a woman who has been defiled, or a prostitute, these he shall not marry. But he shall take as his wife a virgin of his own people, [15] that he may not profane his offspring among his people, for I am the LORD who sanctifies him." (Leviticus 21)*

Proverbs 23:27 describes the prostitute as a deep pit:

> *[27] For a prostitute is a deep pit;*
> *an adulteress is a narrow well. (Proverbs 23)*

The idea here is that she would trap her victim and they will never be able to get out.

Through the prophet Ezekiel, God describes the heart of the prostitute to be sick:

> *[30] "How sick is your heart, declares the Lord*

GOD, because you did all these things, the deeds of a brazen prostitute. (Ezekiel 16)

Ezekiel would go on to describe the punishment of Israel for her prostitution:

[35] "Therefore, O prostitute, hear the word of the LORD: [36] Thus says the Lord GOD, Because your lust was poured out and your nakedness uncovered in your whorings with your lovers, and with all your abominable idols, and because of the blood of your children that you gave to them, [37] therefore, behold, I will gather all your lovers with whom you took pleasure, all those you loved and all those you hated. I will gather them against you from every side and will uncover your nakedness to them, that they may see all your nakedness. [38] And I will judge you as women who commit adultery and shed blood are judged, and bring upon you blood of wrath and jealousy. [39] And I will give you into their hands, and they shall throw down your vaulted chamber and break down your lofty places. They shall strip you of your clothes and take your beautiful jewels and leave you naked and bare. [40] They shall bring up a crowd against you, and they shall stone you and cut you to pieces with their swords. [41] And they shall burn your houses and execute judgments upon you in the sight of many women. I will

*make you stop playing the whore, and you shall
also give payment no more. (Ezekiel 16)*

The words of God through Ezekiel are very strong. God would strip His people bare, expose them to their enemies. He would throw them down from their vaulted bedrooms and break them. He would bring their enemies against them with a sword to cut them to pieces.

Similar words are spoken by Nahum:

> *[4] And all for the countless whorings of the
> prostitute, graceful and of deadly charms,
> who betrays nations with her whorings,
> and peoples with her charms.
> [5] Behold, I am against you,
> declares the LORD of hosts,
> and will lift up your skirts over your face;
> and I will make nations look at your nakedness
> and kingdoms at your shame.
> [6] I will throw filth at you
> and treat you with contempt
> and make you a spectacle. (Nahum 3)*

Nahum prophesies shame and contempt for the prostitute. He made it quite clear that God was against the practice of prostitution in verse 5.

The apostle Paul told the Corinthians that the believer was never to use the services of a prostitute. To do so would be to dishonour the Spirit of Christ who dwelt in them:

> *[15] Do you not know that your bodies are members of Christ? Shall I then take the members of Christ and make them members of a prostitute? Never! [16] Or do you not know that he who is joined to a prostitute becomes one body with her? For, as it is written, "The two will become one flesh." (1 Corinthians 6)*

It is important that we understand that there is forgiveness for those who engage in prostitution. During His ministry on this earth the Lord Jesus encountered prostitutes. We have an example of this in Luke 7:

> *[37] And behold, a woman of the city, who was a sinner, when she learned that he was reclining at table in the Pharisee's house, brought an alabaster flask of ointment, [38] and standing behind him at his feet, weeping, she began to wet his feet with her tears and wiped them with the hair of her head and kissed his feet and anointed them with the ointment. [39] Now when the Pharisee who had invited him saw this, he said to himself, "If this man were a prophet, he would*

have known who and what sort of woman this is who is touching him, for she is a sinner." (Luke 7)

Notice that the people present that day were repulsed at the fact that Jesus allowed this sinful woman to wash His feet. Addressing their reaction to this Jesus said to the them:

[47] Therefore I tell you, her sins, which are many, are forgiven—for she loved much. But he who is forgiven little, loves little." [48] And he said to her, "Your sins are forgiven." (Luke 7)

While the practice of prostitution is clearly something that God detests, He is more than willing to forgive those who repent and come to Him for cleansing.

For Consideration:

What are the different types of prostitution described in the Bible?

Who were the cult prostitutes? What was their role in pagan society?

How did the Moabite women entice Israel to turn from

God?

What words are used in Scripture to describe the practice of prostitution? What does this tell us about how God sees the practice?

How did Jesus treat the "sinful woman" in Luke 7? Does this mean that He approved of her lifestyle?

Consider Paul's words in 1 Corinthians 6:15-16. How does a sexual relationship between a believer and a prostitute bring great dishonour to the Spirit of the Lord Jesus in us?

For Prayer:

There are people in our day caught up in the practice of prostitution. Take a moment to pray that the Lord would set them free from this bondage.

Ask God to open the eyes of these who seek the services of a prostitute to what they are doing and to what God thinks about this sin.

Have you ever fallen into this sin of prostitution or receiving the services of a prostitute? Ask the Lord to forgive and cleanse you?

Consider the attitude of the Lord Jesus toward the sinful woman of Luke 7? Do you have a forgiving and compassionate attitude toward those who practice this trade? Ask God to give you His heart of compassion and forgiveness.

9 - PREMARITAL SEX

In this chapter I would like to touch on what the Bible teaches about a sexual relationship before marriage. One of the first references to this is found in the book of Genesis. The incident relates to a daughter of Jacob and Leah named Dinah.

1 Now Dinah the daughter of Leah, whom she had borne to Jacob, went out to see the women of the land. 2 And when Shechem the son of Hamor the Hivite, the prince of the land, saw her, he seized her and lay with her and humiliated her. (Genesis 34)

Genesis 34:1 tells us that Dinah went out "to see the women of the land." The idea here is that she was befriending the Gentile women of the region. It was while she was with these women that she met a young man by the name of Shechem, a son of the prince of the Hivites. Genesis 34:2 tells us that Shechem "seized" Dinah and lay with her. This indicates that he forced himself on her or possibly raped her. What is particularly important to note here is that in doing so, Shechem humiliated Dinah according to Genesis 34:2.

The word "humiliate" shows us that what took place was unacceptable and would have lasting consequences on the life of Dinah. The Hebrew word can be translated by the words, "afflict" or "oppress" Various translations of the Bible use different words to describe the incident:

"defiled her" – King James Version
"humbled her" – American Standard Version
"humiliated her" –English Standard Version
"violated her" -New International Version, New King James Version

However we translate what took place that day, we see that it was a terrible thing that had lasting implications for Dinah. In fact, Dinah's brothers were so offended by what Shechem had done to their sister that they killed all the men in the city where he lived defending their action by saying: "Should he treat our sister like a prostitute?" (Genesis 34:31).

Listen to the requirements of the Law of Moses regarding a single couple who had sex outside of marriage:

16 "If a man seduces a virgin who is not betrothed and lies with her, he shall give the bride-price for her and make her his wife. 17 If her father utterly refuses to give her to him, he shall pay money equal to the bride-price for virgins. (Exodus 22)

The Old Testament required that if a single man slept with a virgin who was not married, he was to take her to be his wife by paying the bride-price required of the father. If her father refused to allow the man to marry his daughter, the man was still to pay the bride-pride.

Deuteronomy 22 adds another dimension to this law:

28 "If a man meets a virgin who is not betrothed, and seizes her and lies with her, and they are found, 29 then the man who lay with her shall give to the father of the young woman fifty shekels of silver, and she shall be his wife, because he has violated her. He may not divorce her all his days.

Notice in these verses that because he had violated the woman, he was not only to pay the bride-price and take her as his wife, but he could never divorce her (Deuteronomy 22:29). The bride-price was 50 shekels of silver. The general principle here was that if a man had a sexual relationship with a virgin of marriageable age, he was to take her as his wife by paying the dowry and be responsible to her for the rest of his life. A sexual relationship was not to be taken lightly and was only for a couple who were committed to each other for life.

As we examine the teaching of the Bible about premarital sex, it is important that we consider another aspect of this topic. Virginity was held in high regard among young women of the day. When Abraham's servant went to look for a bride for Isaac, one of the qualities he required was that she be a virgin:

> *16 The young woman was very attractive in appearance, a maiden whom no man had known. She went down to the spring and filled her jar and came up. (Genesis 24)*

The priests of the Old Testament were not to marry a woman who was not a virgin:

> *13 And he shall take a wife in her virginity. 14 A widow, or a divorced woman, or a woman who has been defiled, or a prostitute, these he shall not marry. But he shall take as his wife a virgin of his own people, 15 that he may not profane his offspring among his people, for I am the Lord who sanctifies him." (Leviticus 21)*

Notice that a priest who took a wife who was not a virgin would profane his offspring. The children born to this union would be born to a woman who had been defiled by a man who was not their father. The priestly line was not to be profaned in this way.

It may be helpful to examine the story of Amnon and Tamar as found in 2 Samuel 13 to see the shame that was brought upon a woman who lost her virginity outside of marriage. Amnon was David's son. Tamar was the daughter of Absalom and granddaughter to David. 2 Samuel 13 describes Tamar as being a beautiful young woman. Amnon, loved her and wanted to have a sexual relationship with her. He devised a plan to sleep with her by pretending to be sick and asking for her to come to his room to care for him. When they were alone, Amnon asked her to sleep with him. Having more sense than Amnon, Tamar responded:

> 12 She answered him, "No, my brother, do not violate me, for such a thing is not done in Israel; do not do this outrageous thing. 13 As for me, where could I carry my shame? And as for you, you would be as one of the outrageous fools in Israel. Now therefore, please speak to the king, for he will not withhold me from you." (2 Samuel 13)

Tamar's words are important. She reminded Amnon that if he had sex with her he would "violate" her. She reminded him that such a thing "is not done in Israel." She begged him not to do such an "outrageous thing." Tamar went on to tell Amnon that if he carried out his plan, she would have to carry the "shame" and he would be considered by the society to be an "outrageous fool." Her solution was simple. She suggested that Amnon ask the King for permission to marry her. Amnon did not listen to her advice and brought tremendous shame and disgrace on himself and his family.

Tamar understood the purpose of God her sexuality. Her words reveal outrage at the sinful thoughts and desires of Amnon's heart. They also reveal that if he wanted to have a sexual relationship with her, it was only to take place in the context of the lifelong commitment of marriage.

It is interesting to note that the Law of Moses gave instructions on how to deal with a man who claimed that his wife was not a virgin when he married her:

> *13 "If any man takes a wife and goes in to her and then hates her 14 and accuses her of misconduct and brings a bad name upon her, saying, 'I took this woman, and when I came near her, I did not find in her evidence of virginity,' 15 then the father of the young woman and her mother shall take and bring out*

the evidence of her virginity to the elders of the
city in the gate. (Deuteronomy 22)

In this passage we have an example of a man who
married a woman and claimed that after marrying
her he discovered she was not a virgin. This matter
was taken very seriously as it would give the woman
a bad name in the community (Deuteronomy 22:13).
In fact, to protect a woman from the shame of such
an accusation, the woman would present proof of her
virginity to her parents. The parents would keep this
as a guarantee of her purity before marriage.

There is some debate as to what this proof was but the
IVP Bible Background Commentary says this:

Virginity prior to marriage was prized as a
means of insuring that one's children and
heirs were actually one's own. The integrity
of the woman's household was based on her
being able to show proof of her virginity.
The physical evidence demanded in this case
could be either the sheets from the initial
consummation (bloodied by the breaking of
the hymen) or possibly rags used during the
woman's last menstrual period, showing that
she was not pregnant prior to the marriage.
(Walton, John H., Matthews, Victor H.,
Chavalas, Mark W., The IVP Bible Background
Commentary, "Deuteronomy 22:13-21," Cedar

Rapids: Laridian)

If the parents could produce this proof, the husband was to be punished because he had brought shame on a virgin of Israel. He was to be whipped (Deuteronomy 22:18) and fined 100 shekels of silver (Deuteronomy 22:19). This was twice the bride-price for a virgin. He was than to keep her as his wife (Deuteronomy 22:19).

If, however, it was proved that his wife was not a virgin when she married her husband, then the young wife was to be taken to the door of her father's home where she was to be stoned to death (see Deuteronomy 22:20-21). She would pay for her sin and shame would be placed on the home of her father. Her death would purge evil from their midst (Deuteronomy 22:21).

What do we discover from these passages of Scripture? Sex outside of marriage "violated" or "shamed" a woman (and a man as well). It was an outrage in Israelite society. A man who had a sexual relationship with a marriageable young virgin was expected to take her as his wife and provide for her for the rest of her life. A sexual relationship was only to take place in the context of a life long commitment between a man and a woman. It was not to be taken lightly nor were woman simply to be used for pleasure. They were to be respected and honoured.

Virginity was so highly valued that a priest was not

to marry any woman who was not a virgin lest he bring shame on his offspring and defile his priestly line. It was expected that a woman be a virgin when she married a man in Israel. Accusing a woman of not being a virgin when she was married was to bring great shame on her and, if proven false, was punishable by a stiff fine and a whipping. A woman could be stoned to death if it was discovered that she was not a virgin when she married.

In an age were premarital sex is very common, we need to understand the teaching of Scripture afresh. A sexual relationship is to be reserved for marriage and for the partner that God had chosen. In this context, it is pure and holy. Outside of marriage, it is a shame and an outrage.

For Consideration:

What words are used in Scripture to describe a sexual relationship outside of marriage?

What did the Law of Moses require a man to do if he had a sexual relationship with a young unmarried virgin?

What was the punishment for a husband who suggested that his wife was not a virgin when he married her if proven untrue?

What was the punishment for a wife who deceived her husband into thinking that she was a virgin when she married him when this was not the case?

How does the teaching of Scripture about premarital sex provide for a more stable society? How could some of the problems in our society today be resolved by an observance of the principles of Scripture forbidding sex outside of marriage?

For Prayer:

Have you been guilty of having a sexual relationship outside of marriage? Ask the Lord to forgive you for defiling His purpose for sex in a long term and committed relationship between husband and wife.

Consider the attitude that sex is simply to satisfy the desire of the flesh. Ask the Lord to open the eyes of your society to the disrespect and problems this attitude generates.

Ask the Lord to strengthen the resolve of believers and churches around the world to walk in faithfulness to God's purpose for sexual relationships.

10 - NON-CONSENSUAL SEX

Not all sexual relationships are between consenting partners. In this chapter I want to take a moment to examine what the Bible has to say about a forced sexual relationship with non-consenting partner.

Scripture shows us that the problem of rape has existed for a long time. One of the first references to this is found in Genesis 34:

> *1 Now Dinah the daughter of Leah, whom she had borne to Jacob, went out to see the women of the land. 2 And when Shechem the son of Hamor the Hivite, the prince of the land, saw her, he seized her and lay with her and humiliated her. (Genesis 34)*

Notice that Shechem "seized her and lay with her and humiliated her." The idea is that he forced himself on her. We do not have any record of Dinah's response in this situation, but the words used indicate that she was an unwilling partner.

It may also be of importance to note how Shechem felt about Dinah:

> *3 And his soul was drawn to Dinah the daughter of Jacob. He loved the young woman and spoke tenderly to her. 4 So Shechem spoke to his father Hamor, saying, "Get me this girl for my wife." (Genesis 34)*

Shechem loved Dinah and was willing to spend his life with her but he still forced himself on her and humiliated her.

Genesis 34:5 tells us that Shechem "defiled" Dinah by sleeping with her. Listen to the response of Dinah's brothers when they heard what had happened:

> *7 The sons of Jacob had come in from the field as soon as they heard of it, and the men were indignant and very angry, because he had done an outrageous thing in Israel by lying with Jacob's daughter, for such a thing must not be done. (Genesis 34)*

Simeon and Levi, Dinah's brothers were so angry with what Shechem had done that they killed Shechem and all the men in his city in revenge for defiling their sister (see Genesis 34:25-29).

Another example of non-consensual sex is found in 2 Samuel 13. Here Amnon the son of David loved Tamar, his brother's daughter. He hatched a plan to be alone with her and ask her to sleep with him. Though Tamar pleaded with Amnon not to sleep with her, he refused to listen. 2 Samuel 13:14 tell us what happened that day:

> *14 But he would not listen to her, and being stronger than she, he violated her and lay with her. (2 Samuel 13)*

Amnon forced himself on Tamar because he was stronger than her. It is very clear that Tamar was an unwilling partner. She was broken by what had happened that day. 2 Samuel 13:19 describes her response:

> *19 And Tamar put ashes on her head and tore the long robe that she wore. And she laid her hand on her head and went away, crying aloud as she went. (2 Samuel 13)*

Notice the response of Amnon to what happened that day:

> *15 Then Amnon hated her with very great hatred, so that the hatred with which he hated her was greater than the love with which he had loved her. And Amnon said to her, "Get up! Go!" 16 But she said to him, "No, my brother, for this wrong in sending me away is greater than the other that you did to me." But he would not listen to her. 17 He called the young man who served him and said, "Put this woman out of my presence and bolt the door after her." (2 Samuel 13)*

Amnon's "love" (2 Samuel 13:1) turned quickly into an intense hatred after this event. He took no responsibility for her and her humiliation. He simply kicked her out and bolted the door behind her. Amnon would eventually be murdered by Tamar's father for his insult (2 Samuel 13:23-33).

A final example of rape is found in Judges 19. A Levite was traveling through the region of Gibeah in the territory of Benjamin. He found lodging with an old man who provided for his needs. While he was staying with this man, some "worthless fellows" from Benjamin surrounded the house and asked the old man to send out his visitor so that they could have a sexual relationship with him (Judges 19:22). The response of the old man was to protect his visitor. To satisfy these worthless fellows, however, he chose to send out his virgin daughter and the concubine of the Levite (Judges 19:24). Judges 19:25 tells us that these worthless fellows raped and abused the Levite's concubine all night. When the Levite woke up in the morning he found her dead at the doorstep.

When the other tribes found out what had happened to the concubine, they were so angry that they demanded the "worthless fellows" who raped her be handed over. When the tribe of Benjamin refused, they declared war on them. Twenty-five thousand soldiers from Benjamin would perish in that battle.

In each of these cases of rape there was loss of life under tragic circumstances. The attitude of the people of the day toward forced non-consensual sex was to become outraged and angry. In the eyes of the people of those days, to violate a woman through a forced sexual relationship was a sin worthy of death.

Deuteronomy 22:23-29 speaks very directly to this matter of rape or non-consensual sex. The laws of Deuteronomy 22:23-29 can be divided into there parts. Let's examine each part individually.

When The Incident Occurred In The City To An Engaged Woman (Deuteronomy 22:23-24)

23 "If there is a betrothed virgin, and a man meets her in the city and lies with her, 24 then you shall bring them both out to the gate of that city, and you shall stone them to death with stones, the young woman because she did not cry for help though she was in the city, and the man because he violated his neighbor's wife. So you shall purge the evil from your midst.

In Deuteronomy 22:23-24 we have the law of God regarding a case where an engaged woman slept with man in a city. In this case, we have an engaged woman who was by law promised to a husband. In Bible times, an engagement was a legal and binding agreement between a man and a woman. A woman could be charged with adultery if she was unfaithful during this engagement period. In this case, both the man and the woman were to be taken to the gate of the city and stoned to death for adultery.

There was, however, another aspect to this law. What if the woman was raped as an unwilling partner? What if the sexual relationship was not consensual but the man forced himself on the woman? Was the woman guilty if she had not consented to the act? The Law of Moses determined whether the woman was consenting by whether she cried out for help. In a populated city, someone would hear the cry of a woman being raped. If she did not cry out for help, it was assumed that she had consented to the man and was guilty of adultery. In this case, she would be put to death with the man. If she cried out for help, however, she would not be guilty of sin. The law was quite clear that the man would be stoned because he had raped a woman legally bound to another.

When The Incident Occurred In The Country To An Engaged Woman (Deuteronomy 22:25-27)

Deuteronomy 22:25-27 describes a case where an engaged woman was violated in the open country:

> 25 "But if in the open country a man meets a young woman who is betrothed, and the man seizes her and lies with her, then only the man who lay with her shall die. 26 But you shall do nothing to the young woman; she has committed no offense punishable by death. For this case is like that of a man attacking and murdering his neighbor, 27 because he met her in the open country, and though the betrothed young woman cried for help there was no one to rescue her.

In this second case, the assumption was that there was no one around when a man seized and raped her. The fact that the act took place in the country where no one could help was to the woman's favour. The woman would have cried out for help but there was no one to come to her aid. In this case, the woman was an innocent victim. She was not to be punished for she had "committed no offense punishable by death" (Deuteronomy 22:26). As a non-consenting partner, the woman bore no personal responsibility or shame, even through she was defiled.

Single Woman (Deuteronomy 22:28-29)

The final regulations regarding non-consensual sex is found in Deuteronomy 22:28-29:

> *28 "If a man meets a virgin who is not betrothed, and seizes her and lies with her, and they are found, 29 then the man who lay with her shall give to the father of the young woman fifty shekels of silver, and she shall be his wife, because he has violated her. He may not divorce her all his days.*

In this final case, we have a single woman who is not engaged. A man seized her and had a sexual relationship with her. The fact that the man "seized her" indicates that the woman was not consenting to the act. There is no mention here of the location where the event took place. It appears that the law applied if the woman was in the city or in the country. When the sin was revealed, the man was to pay the father of the young woman fifty shekels of silver, take the woman to be his wife, and provide for her all the days of his life. He was not permitted to divorce her. According to Exodus 22:16-17 the law of the Old Testament allowed a father to overrule and if he refused to give his daughter to this man, the man would still have to pay the fine but would not be permitted to marry the woman.

Let me summarize what we have seen in this chapter. Rape or sex with a non-consenting partner is described in the Scripture as an outrage and a violation of the unwilling partner. In the three cases of rape mentioned in Scripture the society was so outraged that they killed the individuals responsible. In the case of the Levite's concubine in Judges 19, the nation was so upset it declared war on the tribe of Benjamin and killed 25,000 men.

If the woman being raped was engaged, the rules of adultery applied, and the rapist was stoned to death. If and engaged woman did not do what she could to call for help, she would be stoned to death with the man. If, however, she cried out for help, though violated by the rapist, she was guiltless and innocent of any crime.

Any man who took sexual advantage of an unwilling single woman was to pay the dowry price to her father, marry her and provide for her for the rest of his life.

For Consideration:

How was rape seen in Bible times? What was the community response to non-consensual sex?

What was the punishment for raping a married or engaged woman according to Deuteronomy 22?

What was the punishment for raping a single woman according to Deuteronomy 22?

Was the person who was raped guilty before the law of God, if she was non-consenting?

Given the sinful nature of the human heart, what can we do to protect ourselves from harm in our society today?

For Prayer:

Do you know someone who has been raped? Take a moment to pray that the Lord would heal that person from the effects of this violation.

Do you know someone who has been raped who feels guilty for what happened even though they were an unwilling partner? Ask the Lord to reassure them of their innocence before Him in this matter.

The woman raped in the open country, through not guilty before the law, may not have been wise to be there by herself. Ask the Lord to give you wisdom so that you do not place yourself in circumstances where you can be hurt.

11 - INCEST

In this chapter, we will take a moment to examine the teaching of Scripture about the practice of incest. Incest is defined as a sexual relationship with a close relative. There are numerous examples of this in the Bible. One of the first such examples is found in the life of Lot. After he and his daughters escaped Sodom and Gomorrah, Lot's daughters began to wonder about their future. Their fiancés had been killed in the judgement of God and they did not know if they would find husbands. They decided on a plan to continue their family line:

[31] And the firstborn said to the younger, "Our father is old, and there is not a man on earth to come in to us after the manner of all the earth. [32] Come, let us make our father drink wine, and we will lie with him, that we may preserve offspring from our father." (Genesis 19)

Lot's daughters became pregnant through a sexual relationship with their father.

The father of Moses was a man by the name of Amram. Amram married his father's sister (his aunt).

[20] Amram took as his wife Jochebed his father's sister, and she bore him Aaron and Moses, the years of the life of Amram being 137 years. (Exodus 6)

We have already mentioned David's son Amnon who raped his brother's sister Tamar in 2 Samuel 13.

In the New Testament, we have the record of John the Baptist being thrown into prison for speaking out against Herod who married his brother's wife:

[17] For it was Herod who had sent and seized John and bound him in prison for the sake of Herodias, his brother Philip's wife, because he had married her. [18] For John had been saying to Herod, "It is not lawful for you to have your brother's wife." (Mark 16)

What was the teaching of the law of God about a sexual relationship with a close relative? Leviticus 18 clearly lays out the purpose of God:

[6] "None of you shall approach any one of his close relatives to uncover nakedness. I am the LORD. [7] You shall not uncover the nakedness of your father, which is the nakedness of your mother; she is your mother, you shall not uncover her nakedness. [8] You shall not uncover the nakedness of your father's wife; it is your father's nakedness. [9] You shall not uncover the nakedness of your sister, your father's daughter or your mother's daughter, whether brought up in the family or in another home. [10] You shall not uncover the nakedness of your son's daughter or of your daughter's daughter, for their nakedness is your own nakedness. [11] You shall not uncover the nakedness of your father's wife's daughter, brought up in your father's family, since she is your sister. [12] You shall not uncover the nakedness of your father's sister; she is your father's relative. [13] You shall not uncover the nakedness of your mother's sister, for she is your mother's relative. [14] You shall not uncover the nakedness of your father's brother, that is, you shall not approach his wife; she is your aunt. [15] You shall not uncover the nakedness of your daughter-in-law; she is your son's wife, you shall not uncover her nakedness. [16] You shall not uncover the nakedness of your brother's wife; it is your brother's nakedness. [17] You shall not uncover the nakedness of a woman and of her daughter, and you shall

not take her son's daughter or her daughter's daughter to uncover her nakedness; they are relatives; it is depravity. [18] And you shall not take a woman as a rival wife to her sister, uncovering her nakedness while her sister is still alive. (Leviticus 18)

Leviticus 18 describes the sin of incest as the sin of having a sexual relationship with a close relative. This included the following relations:

A father (verse 7)
A mother (verse 7)
A father's wife (verse 8) - whether she was one's mother or not
A sister (verse 9) - who lived with them or in another home
A grandchild (verse 10)
A step sister (verse 11)
An aunt (verses 12, 13)
An uncle (verse 14)
An uncle's wife (verse 14)
A daughter-in-law (verse 15)
A sister-in law (verse 16)
A woman and her daughter (verse 17)
A woman and her sister (verse 18)

Leviticus 20 prescribes the punishment for those who committed incest. If a man had a sexual relationship with his father's wife both partners were to be put to death.

> *[11] If a man lies with his father's wife, he has uncovered his father's nakedness; both of them shall surely be put to death; their blood is upon them. (Leviticus 20)*

If the sexual relationship was with a daughter-in-law again both partners were to be killed:

> *[12] If a man lies with his daughter-in-law, both of them shall surely be put to death; they have committed perversion; their blood is upon them. (Leviticus 20)*

For sleeping with a woman and her daughter all three partners were to be burned with fire:

> *[14] If a man takes a woman and her mother also, it is depravity; he and they shall be burned with fire, that there may be no depravity among you. (Leviticus 20)*

The man who slept with his sister was to be cut off from the people of God. This may imply being banished from the nation of Israel or it may also imply that that person was to be killed:

[17] "If a man takes his sister, a daughter of his father or a daughter of his mother, and sees her nakedness, and she sees his nakedness, it is a disgrace, and they shall be cut off in the sight of the children of their people. He has uncovered his sister's nakedness, and he shall bear his iniquity. (Leviticus 20)

Finally, if the sexual relationship was with an aunt or a sister-in-law, they would be placed under the curse of God and die childless with no one to carry on their family name:

[19] You shall not uncover the nakedness of your mother's sister or of your father's sister, for that is to make naked one's relative; they shall bear their iniquity. [20] If a man lies with his uncle's wife, he has uncovered his uncle's nakedness; they shall bear their sin; they shall die childless. [21] If a man takes his brother's wife, it is impurity. He has uncovered his brother's nakedness; they shall be childless. (Leviticus 20)

In Deuteronomy 27, Moses commanded the people to participate in a ceremony when they arrived in the region of Canaan. After crossing the Jordan River, the Levites were to stand on Mount Gerizim and speak to the people in a loud voice reminding them of the curses of God. The people were to acknowledge these curses and place themselves under obligation to walk in God's way. Notice Deuteronomy 27:20, 22, 23:

[20] "'Cursed be anyone who lies with his father's wife, because he has uncovered his father's nakedness.' And all the people shall say, 'Amen.' (Deuteronomy 27)

[22] "'Cursed be anyone who lies with his sister, whether the daughter of his father or the daughter of his mother.' And all the people shall say, 'Amen.' (Deuteronomy 27)

[23] "'Cursed be anyone who lies with his mother-in-law.' And all the people shall say, 'Amen.' (Deuteronomy 27)

As the people of God entered the Promised Land they were to acknowledge that that curse of God would be on them if they were guilty of the sexual sin of incest.

The prophet Amos made it clear that these prohibited sexual relationships were not merely a sin against each other but also profaned the name of God:

[7] those who trample the head of the poor into

the dust of the earth
and turn aside the way of the afflicted;
a man and his father go in to the same girl,
so that my holy name is profaned; (Amos 2)

We have a record in 1 Corinthians 5:1 of a man connected with the church in Corinth whom Paul reprimanded for having a sexual relation with his father's wife:

[5:1] It is actually reported that there is sexual immorality among you, and of a kind that is not tolerated even among pagans, for a man has his father's wife. [2] And you are arrogant! Ought you not rather to mourn? Let him who has done this be removed from among you. [3] For though absent in body, I am present in spirit; and as if present, I have already pronounced judgment on the one who did such a thing. (1 Corinthians 5)

Notice the response of the apostle Paul to this incestuous relationship. He appears to be shocked that this had happened. He speaks of this relationship as being sexually immoral. He is angered that the church of Corinth had done nothing about this problem. He pronounced his judgement on the man and told the believers to remove him from their church.

It is quite clear from these verses that a sexual relationship with a close relative is not the purpose of God. Such relationships were forbidden and under the Old Testament law were punishable in many cases by death. The New Testament also considers incest to be a sin and those guilty of this sin were to be reprimanded and, in some cases, removed from fellowship.

For Consideration:

Did the Old Testament saints always walk in God's purpose for their sexuality? Give some examples of people in Bible times who disobeyed God's law about incest.

What was the punishment for incest in the Law of Moses? What does this tell us about how serious God viewed this matter?

How did the law of God about incest protect families and the society? What problems would be the result of breaking this law in families and in society in general?

To what extent is incest and sexual abuse of close relatives a problem in your society?

For Prayer:

Thank the Lord for His grace and forgiveness in the lives of Old Testament saints even when they fell short of God's standard.

Ask the Lord to give us safe family relations free from sexual abuse and violence.

Do you know someone who has been sexually abused by a family member? Take a moment to pray that the Lord would heal the pain of this abuse and bring deep conviction of sin to the perpetrator.

12 - HOMOSEXUALITY

We come now to the practice of homosexuality. In the Old Testament, there does not appear to be a specific word used for this practice. It is described, however, as one who lies with a male as with a woman (see Leviticus 18:22 and 20:13).

In the New Testament, the apostle Paul uses two Greek words to describe homosexuality. The first is found in 1 Corinthians 6:9. Here the apostle uses the word "malakos" to refer to a man. The word "malakos" means "soft to the touch." It is translated in the King James Version by the word "effeminate".

The second word used to describe homosexuality in the New Testament is found in 1 Timothy 1:10. The Greek word used is "arsenokoites". "Arsenokoites" comes from the word "arsen" meaning a male and "koite" meaning a bed. The word "koite" is used in Hebrews 13:4 to speak of the marriage bed. In Romans 13:13 "koite" is translated in the King James Version as "chambering" or sexual immorality in the English Standard Version. "Arsenokoites" refers to a man who sleeps with another man and has a sexual relationship with him. What is true for men here is also true for women. Homosexuality is the practice of having a sexual relationship with a member of the same sex.

Homosexuality is nothing new. We have several references to the practice in the Bible. Probably the first recorded occurrence is found in Genesis 19. Here we have the story of God preparing to destroy the city of Sodom where Abraham's cousin Lot and his family lived. Because of the prayer of Abraham, God sent His angels to remove Lot and his family from the city before it was destroyed.

The angels were invited to stay with Lot. When the men of the city discovered that Lot had visitors they surrounded his house and demanded that he send the men out to them:

> *5 And they called to Lot, "Where are the men who came to you tonight? Bring them out to us, that we may know them." 6 Lot went out to the men at the entrance, shut the door after him, 7 and said, "I beg you, my brothers, do not act so wickedly (Genesis 19)*

Notice in verse 5 that the men wanted to know these visitors. The word "know" has a variety of meanings. It can simply mean to become acquainted with an individual. It is also used however, to speak of a sexual relationship. We have an example of this in Genesis 4:1:

1 And Adam knew Eve his wife; and she conceived and bore Cain, saying, "I have gotten a man with the help of the Lord." (Genesis 4)

The result of Adam "knowing" his wife was that she became pregnant.

In the case of the men who surrounded the home of Lot in Sodom we have every reason to believe that their intentions were not simply to become acquainted with Lot's visitors. The context makes this very clear. Notice how Lot went to the door of his house and begged the men not to "act so wickedly." Lot knew that the intention of these men was to sexually abuse his visitors. In fact, Lot even offered his two daughters who had never "known a man" to them to satisfy their sexual desires. The men of the city refused Lot's daughters and attempted to break down the door of his house to get at his visitors (Genesis 19:9). The angels in Lot's home struck these men with blindness. We understand from this the moral climate of the city of Sodom and why the Lord wanted to judge the city.

A similar incident happened in Judges 19. Here we have the story of a Levite and his concubine traveling through the region of Benjamin. While enjoying the hospitality of an old man in the city, some "worthless men" surrounded the house and demanded that the old man bring out his guest so that they could know him:

> *22 As they were making their hearts merry, behold, the men of the city, worthless fellows, surrounded the house, beating on the door. And they said to the old man, the master of the house, "Bring out the man who came into your house, that we may know him." 23 And the man, the master of the house, went out to them and said to them, "No, my brothers, do not act so wickedly; since this man has come into my house, do not do this vile thing. (Judges 19)*

Notice again that the old man begged the "worthless fellows" not to act so wickedly (verse 23). He too offered the men his virgin daughter and the concubine of the Levite. Unlike the men in Sodom, these "worthless fellows" took the man's daughter and the concubine of his guest, abused her sexually all night and left her dead on the doorstep. What is important to note in this context, however, is that the "worthless fellows" mentioned here were looking to have a sexual relationship with the male guest. It was him they wanted to "know."

Admittedly, these are extreme examples. Homosexuality is not the only issue in these verses. Disrespect for foreigners, rape, murder and violence are also very much part of the sins referred to here. I cite these two examples, however, to show that the desire for a same-sex relationship goes back even to Bible times.

While the above examples of homosexual desire are in the context of rape and violence, what does the Bible say about homosexual relationships between consenting adults? Let's take a moment to examine the Law of God in the Old Testament and what it says about consenting homosexual relationships.

> *22 You shall not lie with a male as with a woman; it is an abomination. (Leviticus 18)*

Leviticus 18:22 forbids a man to "lie with a male as with a woman." The word translated "lie" here is the Hebrew word "ekobet" The word is defined by the AMG Complete Word Study Dictionary as follows:

> *Ekobet: A feminine noun referring to intercourse; copulation. It refers to the act of sexual intercourse (Lev 18:20; Nu 5:20) (Baker, Warren; Carpenter, Eugene: AMG Word Study*

Dictionary Old Testament, "7903. Ekobet,"
Cedar Rapids: Laridian)

What the law of Moses forbade here was a sexual relationship between two males. Notice also that the practice of homosexuality is described in Leviticus 18:22 as "an abomination."

Leviticus 20:13 take this law a step further but prescribing the punishment for homosexual relations:

> *13 If a man lies with a male as with a woman, both of them have committed an abomination; they shall surely be put to death; their blood is upon them. (Leviticus 20)*

Notice again that a sexual relationship between two men is described as an "abomination." The punishment for this act was death according to the Law of Moses.

As we come to the New Testament, the Apostle Paul, speaks to the Romans about how men and women turned from God and "became fools" (Romans 1:22). Because they refused God and His ways, God gave them up "in the lust of their hearts to impurity, to the dishonoring of their bodies among themselves" (Romans 1:24). The words Paul uses here are important. These individuals were given over to impurity and the dishonoring of their bodies among themselves. What was this impurity that dishonored their bodies? Paul goes on in verse 26 to explain:

> *26 For this reason God gave them up to dishonorable passions. For their women exchanged natural relations for those that are contrary to nature; 27 and the men likewise gave up natural relations with women and were consumed with passion for one another, men committing shameless acts with men and receiving in themselves the due penalty for their error. (Romans 1)*

It was homosexual acts that dishonoured their bodies. These homosexual passions are described by Paul in verse 26 as being "dishonorable". Notice that while the Old Testament laws seem to focus on male homosexuality, Paul reminds us that females are also guilty of the same sin (see Romans 1:26).

Paul describes women who gave up natural relations with those that were contrary to nature. He explains what he means by this in verse 27 when he begins the verse with the word "likewise". He went on in verse 27 to describe men who were consumed with passion for other men resulting in "shameless acts". What was true for men was also true for women. Homosexual acts, whether between consenting males or females, according to Paul, were shameful and dishonoured the body. More than this, however, Paul reminds those who practice homosexuality that they would receive "the due penalty for their error" (Romans 1:27).

Paul would go on further in 1 Corinthians 6:9 to say:

> *9 Or do you not know that the unrighteous will not inherit the kingdom of God? Do not be deceived: neither the sexually immoral, nor idolaters, nor adulterers, nor men who practice homosexuality, 10 nor thieves, nor the greedy, nor drunkards, nor revilers, nor swindlers will inherit the kingdom of God. 11 And such were some of you. But you were washed, you were sanctified, you were justified in the name of the Lord Jesus Christ and by the Spirit of our God. (1 Corinthians 6)*

In this passage, Paul lists sins that make a person unfit for the kingdom of God. While he reminds us in verse 11 that there is forgiveness for all these sins, these practices had no place in the lives of those who belonged to Christ. Notice, for our purposes, the reference to "men who practice homosexuality" in verse 9. In other words, there was no place for the practice of homosexual relationships among those who belonged to the kingdom of God. It was a practice that offended God and one that must be confessed as sin.

As the apostle writes to Timothy in 1 Timothy 1, he explained to him the purpose of the Law of God:

> *8 Now we know that the law is good, if one uses it lawfully, 9 understanding this, that the law is not laid down for the just but for the lawless and disobedient, for the ungodly and sinners, for the unholy and profane, for those who strike their fathers and mothers, for murderers, 10 the sexually immoral, men who practice homosexuality, enslavers, liars, perjurers, and whatever else is contrary to sound doctrine (1 Timothy 1)*

Paul told Timothy that the law of God was intended to correct those who were lawless, disobedient, ungodly, sinners, unholy and profane (verse 9). He gives examples of these people in verses 9 and 10. Included among these is a reference to the "sexually immoral, men who practice homosexuality." The law of God was given to correct a variety of sins among which was the sin of homosexuality, which was "contrary to sound doctrine" (verse 10).

Finally, in Jude 7 we read:

> *7 just as Sodom and Gomorrah and the surrounding cities, which likewise indulged in sexual immorality and pursued unnatural*

desire, serve as an example by undergoing a punishment of eternal fire.

Jude tells us that Sodom and Gomorrah indulged in sexual immorality and pursued "unnatural desires." While there are a variety of possible meanings for this, we do know that homosexuality was one of the sins of Sodom in the days of Lot. Paul refers to homosexual desire to be an "unnatural desire" in Romans 1:26-27. Homosexuality is likely included in this reference to the sins of Sodom and Gomorrah. What is important for us to note here is that Sodom and Gomorrah were to be punished by eternal fire as an example to those who indulged in sexual immorality and pursued unnatural desire.

While homosexuality is becoming much more acceptable in our society, the Bible's teaching is quite clear. Scripture uses strong language to speak about homosexuality and what God thinks about it. Those who want to walk in obedience to the teaching of Scripture must learn to deal with homosexual impulses and confess any homosexual activity as sin before God. This is not an accepted position in our society. My purpose, in this study, is to reveal the teaching of Scripture and challenge those who claim to be Christians to live by its standard.

For Consideration:

What words are used in Scripture to describe a sexual relationship between two partners of the same sex.

What was the Old Testament punishment for homosexual relations?

While homosexuality is not punishable by death in the New Testament, how did the apostle Paul view the practice?

Homosexuality is culturally accepted in many societies today. Does society's acceptance of homosexual relations change the position of the Bible on this matter or how God views its practice?

Consider how Jesus treated prostitutes and the woman caught in adultery? What does this teach us about how we need to treat homosexuals in our day? Is it possible to treat people with respect and dignity and still disagree with their lifestyle?

For Prayer:

Do you have friends who are homosexual? Ask the Lord to minister to them and reveal His purpose to them.

Do you know believers who are struggling with homosexuality? Ask God to strengthen them and give them grace to walk in His purpose for their lives.

Ask the Lord to give you grace to love and respect homosexuals as Jesus loved and respected the people He encountered while He was on the earth. Ask Him for grace to hold fast to the teaching of His Word about homosexuality while still loving those who are caught up in the practice.

13 - TRANSGENDERISM

In this chapter I would like to touch on the issue of transgenderism. Transgenderism is defined by the Oxford dictionary as follows:

A state or condition in which a person's identity does not conform unambiguously to conventional ideas of male or female gender. (https://en.oxforddictionaries.com/definition/transgenderism)

The key to understanding transgenderism seems to be in the word "identify." The transgender person does not clearly identify himself or herself with the sex with which they were born. The term is broad, and the expression of transgenderism is varied. Transgenders may feel free to identify with both sexes throughout their lives. Some transgenders express their identity by dressing and acting like their preferred gender. Still others undergo surgical procedures to change their sex organs. Gender, for the transgender person is not defined by biology.

The issue of transgenderism has caused a great deal of confusion in western society. Should a person who was born male but identifies as a female use a female washroom or a male washroom? How are transgenders to be identified on their passports or birth certificates? How are we to address an individual who does not identify with the "he" or "she" pronouns. Can we say that a child is male or female simply because of their biology? These are questions western society is now trying to sort out as it learns to deal with the transgenderism of our day. It is not my purpose to discuss the sociological issues related to transgenderism. I do, however, want to examine some Biblical principles related to this important issue of our day.

As we begin, let me say that Jesus treated all people with respect and dignity. He did this sometimes to the frustration of the religious leaders of the day who saw Him as a friend of sinners:

> *34 The Son of Man has come eating and drinking, and they say, "Look at him! A glutton and a drunkard, a friend of tax collectors and sinners!" (Luke 7)*

When Jesus went to the home of a Pharisee in Luke 7, "a woman of the city" came in with a flask of ointment and anointed His feet. Listen to the response of the Pharisee who saw this:

> *39 Now when the Pharisee who had invited him saw this, he said to himself. "If this man were a prophet, he would have known who and what sort of woman this is who is touching him, for she is a sinner." (Luke 7)*

In response, Jesus, seeing her sorrow and repentant heart, forgave her sin. He did not judge her as the Pharisee did. They wanted nothing to do with her. Jesus, however, accepted her and forgave her sin. He did not condone her actions but respected her as a person. We need to have this attitude of Jesus in our relationship with people who differ from us.

Having said this, we need now to examine the teaching of Scripture as it pertains to this matter of transgenderism. Let's begin with how the Bible defines male and female.

Genesis 1:26-27 speaking of the creation of "man" says the following:

> *26 Then God said, "Let us make man in our image, after our likeness. And let them have*

dominion over the fish of the sea and over the birds of the heavens and over the livestock and over all the earth and over every creeping thing that creeps on the earth."

27 So God created man in his own image,
in the image of God he created him;
male and female he created them. (Genesis 1)

There are three Hebrew words used in these two verses. In Genesis 1:26 we read that God said: "Let us make man." The Hebrew word used for man is the word "adam". This word refers to humans in general. In other words, God said: "Let us make humankind."

When God made humanity, He chose to make two kinds of humans. Genesis 1:27 tells us that He made a male and a female. The word for male is the word "zakar" and speaks or a man or one whose sex is male. It is never used to speak of a female. The word for female is the word "neqebah" and is only used to speak of a person whose sex is female.

Listen to how the King James Version of the Bible translates Genesis 5:2:

2 Male and female created he them; and blessed them, and called their name Adam, in the day when they were created. (KJV, Genesis 5)

God created "adam" (human beings) with both a male and a female sex.

We see than that it was God's purpose to create two separate sexes. The question we now must ask ourselves is how these sexes are defined in the Bible. To answer this, let's begin with Genesis 17:10-11:

> *9 And God said to Abraham, "As for you, you shall keep my covenant, you and your offspring after you throughout their generations. 10 This is my covenant, which you shall keep, between me and you and your offspring after you: Every male among you shall be circumcised. 11 You shall be circumcised in the flesh of your foreskins, and it shall be a sign of the covenant between me and you. (Genesis 17)*

Genesis 17 speaks about the covenant God established between Himself and Abraham's descendants. This covenant was for Abraham and his offspring through out their generations (verse 9). In Genesis 17:11 God told His people that they were to cut off the foreskin of every male in the land as a sign of their covenant relationship with Him. The word used to describe those who needed to be circumcised is the Hebrew word "zakar" which refers to males only. A male is described, therefore, as one who has a foreskin. The difference between a male and a female had to do in part with their sex organs. It was a biological distinction.

In Genesis 6:19 God commanded Noah to bring the animals in the ark. God made it clear that he was to bring both male (zakar) and female (neqebah). The only way Noah had to distinguish male and female was to examine the biological characteristics of these animals to determine their sex.

Throughout the Old Testament, there is a distinction made between male and female. In Exodus 13:12-13 God required that a firstborn male animal to be given to Him. Every firstborn male child was to be redeemed at a cost to the parents. God required a distinction between male and female animals in the offerings His people brought. The Passover Lamb was to be a male lamb (Exodus 12:1-5). Only a male lamb could be offered as a burnt offering (Leviticus 1:3). The Israelites, however, could offer either a male or female animal for a peace offering (Leviticus 3:1). There was also a distinction made in the number of days a woman required for purification after the birth of her child. If a mother had a male child, she was unclean for seven days (Leviticus 12:2). If she had a female child, she was unclean for fourteen days (Leviticus 12:5). What is important for us to note is that the Lord God required His people to make a distinction between male and female. The Lord had different requirements for each sex and so it was important that God's people recognize the difference.

We have seen in Genesis 17:10 that males are described as those who have a foreskin. In Genesis 3:16 we have a description of "woman". Speaking to Eve God says:

> *16 To the woman he said,*
> *"I will surely multiply your pain in childbearing;*
> *in pain you shall bring forth children.*
> *Your desire shall be contrary to your husband,*
> *but he shall rule over you." (Genesis 3)*

This verse makes is quite clear that a woman is one who has been created with the ability to bear children. This again shows us that sex is defined by biology.

The Bible defines human beings in terms of being male or female. This distinction is based on their biological differences. Let's take this a step further. Speaking to Job, the Lord God said:

> *8 "Or who shut in the sea with doors*
> *when it burst out from the womb,*
> *9 when I made clouds its garment*
> *and thick darkness its swaddling band,*
> *10 and prescribed limits for it*
> *and set bars and doors,*
> *11 and said, 'Thus far shall you come, and no farther,*
> *and here shall your proud waves be stayed'? (Job*

38)

Notice what the Lord God is saying here. God compares the sea to a baby that has come out of the womb. God wrapped it up in clouds like clothes and prescribed a limit for it saying: "Thus far shall you come, and no farther." God created the sea with its limits. He has a purpose and intent in what He creates. He limits His creation to that purpose. He makes no mistake when He creates us as we are.

Speaking to the Romans, the apostle Paul said:

> *20 But who are you, O man, to answer back to God? Will what is molded say to its molder, "Why have you made me like this?" 21 Has the potter no right over the clay, to make out of the same lump one vessel for honorable use and another for dishonorable use? (Romans 9)*

Some time ago I was listening to a young man who identified as a woman, weeping over the fact that he was not born a female. There are those who are angry with God for how He created them. For those of us who want to live in submission to God, however, we must come to understand that God's purpose is right and good. Listen to the words of the Psalmist in Psalm 139:

13 For you formed my inward parts;
you knitted me together in my mother's womb.
14 I praise you, for I am fearfully and
wonderfully made.
Wonderful are your works;
my soul knows it very well.
15 My frame was not hidden from you,
when I was being made in secret,
intricately woven in the depths of the earth.
16 Your eyes saw my unformed substance;
in your book were written, every one of them,
the days that were formed for me,
when as yet there was none of them. (Psalm
139)

It was God who formed us in our mother's womb. The Psalmist declared that this work of God was wonderful. God knows every day that is before us and the purpose He has for us in each of those days. He made no mistake in creating us as we are. We were born male or female in God's purpose and plan.

It is the intention of God that we walk in the purpose for which He created us. Writing to the Corinthians the apostle Paul says:

20 Each one should remain in the condition in
which he was called. 21 were you a bondservant
when called? Do not be concerned about it. (But

if you can gain your freedom, avail yourself of the opportunity) (1 Corinthians 7)

What is the apostle telling the Corinthians? He is telling them that they were to learn to be content with where the Lord had put them. If they were servants when they came to Christ, then be the best servants they could be as a Christian. The principle applies to this subject of transgenderism as well. Were you created male, then live as such. Were you created female, then learn to be all that God has called you to be as a female.

24 So brothers, in whatever condition each was called, there let him remain with God. (1 Corinthians 7)

We are not to seek to change what God has ordained and created. Instead, we are to learn to walk faithfully in what He has given us to bear. He will give strength and wisdom to be faithful to His call on our lives.

It is in this context that we should understand the teaching of the Law of Moses in Deuteronomy 22:5:

5 "A woman shall not wear a man's garment, nor shall a man put on a woman's cloak, for whoever does these things is an abomination to the Lord your God. (Deuteronomy 22)

There have been times when I have been out with my wife and the weather has been quite cold. I have sometimes given her my coat to wear to keep warm. I believe this to be right and godly. When the Bible tells us that a woman should not wear a man's garment, it is not speaking about such acts of kindness or charity. The practice of wearing clothes belonging to the opposite sex may have been prevalent in the pagan fertility religious of the day and as such God wanted a separation from this false religion. Beyond this, however, was the rejection of what God had created His people to be. For a man to dress and live as a female was to show discontent with the sex God had given him. This according to Deuteronomy 22:5 was an abomination to the Lord God.

While we have no clear example of transgenderism in the Bible, we do have some principles by which the believer is called to live. God created us male and female. Male and female are defined in biological terms in Scripture. God's people were to regularly distinguish between male and female humans and animals in their service of their Creator. It is the understanding of Scripture that what God creates is good and right. The believer is to live in surrender to God and His purpose.

I am not suggesting that this will be easy for those who are inclined to be transgender. Nor am I suggesting that all men are "macho", outdoor sportsmen. Genesis 25, 27 describes the difference between Jacob and Esau:

> *[26] Afterward his brother came out with his hand holding Esau's heel, so his name was called Jacob. Isaac was sixty years old when she bore them. [27] When the boys grew up, Esau was a skillful hunter, a man of the field, while Jacob was a quiet man, dwelling in tents. [28] Isaac loved Esau because he ate of his game, but Rebekah loved Jacob. (Genesis 25)*

Genesis 25 describes Esau as a skillful hunter and a man of the field. Jacob, on the other hand was a quiet man who stayed home. While Esau was a out hunting, Isaac was home with his mother cooking. Esau and Jacob were very different in personality and preference. Jacob was loved by his mom and a favourite child of hers. Esau, on the other hand had a better relationship with his father. These differences should not go unnoticed. Jacob's preference to stay home with his mother and cook did not make him any less a man. He did not sin by preferring to be with his mother. Not all males will enjoy the same things. Nor will all females have the same personality. We need to allow preferences and personality differences among those of the same sex without looking down on them. Sometimes we have culturally defined roles we feel cannot be challenged. While Jacob did not enjoy what was culturally perceived to be male activities, he never denounced the sex of his birth.

There is another detail we need to examine regarding the difference between Jacob and Esau. Listen to what Jacob told his mother in Genesis 27:

[11] But Jacob said to Rebekah his mother, "Behold, my brother Esau is a hairy man, and I am a smooth man. (Genesis 27)

Notice that Jacob who loved to cook and be with his mother was a smooth and relatively hairless man. Esau, the one who loved to hunt was a hairy man. There was a difference between these two sons. A hairy chest and arms are generally considered to be a male characteristic. Jacob did not demonstrate these characteristics. His appearance was less "masculine" than his brother. Let me emphasize, again, however, that despite his preferences and appearance, Jacob did not question his masculinity. He would live as a man and go on to marry and have a family.

What have we learned in this chapter? We see that God made both male and female. The difference between male and female was defined by biological differences. God expected that His people make a distinction between the sexes in their sacrifices and lifestyle. Men were not to dress as females. While not all men and women are the same, God expects that we learn to accept our biological distinctives and live as He created us.

For Consideration:

How did the Lord Jesus treat those who were different from Him? How are we to treat those who do not see things as we see them?

How does the Bible define male and female?

Why is it important that we accept what God has created and how He has created us? Can we truly be all that God intends us to be if we do not accept His purpose?

Should we expect that all males will enjoy the same things or that all females will be the same? Are all our cultural definitions of what it means to be male and female true?

To what extent is transgenderism an issue in your society?

For Prayer:

Take a moment to thank the Lord for how He has created both male and female. Thank Him for the differences and how those differences work together.

Thank the Lord that He is a good God who knows exactly what He is doing. Ask Him to give you grace to accept who He has made you to be.

Have you been struggling with how the Lord has made you? Ask Him for strength to accept who He has made you to be?

Do you have friends or loved ones who are transgender? Take a moment to pray that the Lord would reveal His purpose clearly to them. Ask the Lord to strengthen them to live in His purpose for their lives.

14 - PORNOGRAPHY, LUST AND MODESTY

In this chapter I want to address what the Bible has to say about pornography and lust. Pornography and lust are very closely related. Pornography is generally defined as pictures or writing that are designed to stimulate sexual excitement or passion. The object of that passion, however, is not always one's marriage partner. We have an example of this in the book of Ezekiel. Listen to what the Lord says about His own people:

12 She lusted after the Assyrians, governors and commanders, warriors clothed in full armor, horsemen riding on horses, all of them desirable young men. 13 And I saw that she was defiled; they both took the same way. 14 But she carried her whoring further. She saw men portrayed on the wall, the images of the Chaldeans portrayed in vermilion, 15 wearing belts on their waists, with flowing turbans on their heads, all of them having the appearance of officers, a likeness of Babylonians whose native land was Chaldea. 16 When she saw them, she lusted after them and sent messengers to them in Chaldea. 17 And the Babylonians came to her into the bed of love, and they defiled her with their whoring lust. And after she was defiled by them, she turned from them in disgust. 18 When she carried on her whoring so openly and flaunted her nakedness, I turned in disgust from her, as I had turned in disgust from her sister. (Ezekiel 23)

This passage from Ezekiel is quite graphic but what it says is important in our discussion of pornography. Notice what it is happening here. Judah saw "desirable young men" –Assyrian governors, commanders and warriors dressed in their full armour and found herself lusting after them (verse 12). Watching them stirred her sexual desire. In verse 14 she looked at pictures hanging on the wall of Chaldeans officers dressed in vermilion (bright red). They were wearing belts and flowing turbans. Her response to these pictures is described in verse 16 –she lusted after them and sent messengers to have them come to her. When they came to her she took them "into the bed of love, and they defiled her with their whoring lust" (verse 17). Notice also that Israel not only looked at and lusted over these men whose pictures were hanging on the wall, but she too "flaunted her nakedness" for others (verse 18).

Note the response of God to this pornography and lust. He "turned in disgust from her" (Ezekiel 23:18). We see here how these pictures and images stirred up sexual passion in the people of God. That passion caused her to lust after those whose pictures and images she saw portrayed on the wall.

In Job 31, Job made a commitment before God:

> *1 "I have made a covenant with my eyes;*
> *how then could I gaze at a virgin? (Job 31)*

The word translated "gaze" here has the idea of observing or paying attention to a certain object or person. To gaze has a sense of lingering on what one sees. The King James Version translates the phrase with "think upon a maiden." It is to allow one's thoughts to wander as one allows the eyes to linger. The New Living Translation translates "to look with lust upon a young woman." The idea is quite clear in Job 31. Job would not allow his eyes to linger on a young woman so that he began to lust after her.

Job's words are important. He made a covenant with

his eyes. We are not talking here about Job having a sexual relationship with this young woman. Job's commitment is to his eyes and heart. He refused even to allow his eyes the privilege of lingering on what was not his. He refused to allow his mind to think about what it would be like to have what was not his. Job's commitment was to keep his eyes and mind free of lustful thoughts and desires. To do this he made it his principle in life not to allow himself to "gaze" or "think upon" a young woman.

We read in Genesis 39 about Potiphar's wife.

> *6 ... Now Joseph was handsome in form and appearance. 7 And after a time his master's wife cast her eyes on Joseph and said, "Lie with me." (Genesis 39)*

Joseph had been sold into slavery and worked for Potiphar in Egypt. Potiphar's wife "cast her eye on Joseph". Genesis 39:6 tells us that "Joseph was handsome in form and appearance." This is likely what caught the attention of Potiphar's wife. She saw him and began to lust after him. She allowed herself the privilege of "gazing" on him. This stirred up her sexual desires and so she made a request that he sleep with her (verse 7).

We are quite aware of the commandment of God in Exodus 20:14: "You shall not commit adultery." We also need to uphold the commandment that says: "You shall not covet your neighbour's wife" (Exodus 20:17).

The word covet is not often used in our modern day. The Hebrew word means to have a passionate desire or to lust after something. In other words, Exodus 20:17 is telling us that we are not to lust over our neighbour's wife. We are not to "gaze" upon her with passionate desire. While the commandment of Exodus 20:14 prohibits a sexual relationship with a woman or man outside of marriage, Exodus 20:17 prohibits even allowing our hearts and minds to lust after them. God expects that we quickly destroy any lustful thoughts in our hearts or minds.

Jesus would expand on this Old Testament commandment in Matthew 5:

> 27 "You have heard that it was said, 'You shall not commit adultery.' 28 But I say to you that everyone who looks at a woman with lustful intent has already committed adultery with her in his heart. (Matthew 5)

Jesus makes is clear that for a married man to covet or to look at a woman other than his wife with lustful intent is to commit adultery in our heart. What is true of a married man committing adultery is also true for single man looking with lustful intent in his eyes. The only thing worse than committing sin in our heart is physically acting out on those lustful impulses.

What we need to understand from this is that the Lord is concerned for our hearts as well as our bodies. His desire is that we be pure not only in body but also in thought and mind. When we, like Judah gaze on the images of "desirable young men" and allow ourselves to lust after them, we have defiled our heart and mind. When we allow ourselves to "gaze on a young virgin" we defile our thoughts. God wants us to be free from such burdensome passions. Pornography stirs up the sexual passions in ways that God does not intend and defiles our mind and heart.

Closely connected to this is the challenge of Scripture to live with modesty in our appearance. The apostle Paul compares the church to the physical body. Listen to what he told the church in Corinth in 1 Corinthians 12:

> *21 The eye cannot say to the hand, "I have no need of you," nor again the head to the feet, "I have no need of you." 22 On the contrary, the parts of the body that seem to be weaker are indispensable, 23 and on those parts of the body that we think less honorable we bestow the greater honor, and our unpresentable parts are treated with greater modesty, 24 which our more presentable parts do not require. But God has so composed the body, giving greater honor to the part that lacked it, (1 Corinthians 12)*

Notice particularly in verse 23 that the apostle says: "our unpresentable parts are treated with greater modesty." For Paul there were parts of our body that were "unpresentable" and needed to be treated with "greater modesty." While all parts of the body are important and serve a very important need, not all are visible and some in fact need to be unexposed.

In Genesis 9 we read that Noah drank wine and became drunk. In his drunkenness, he fell asleep naked in his tent. When his son Ham discovered him, he told his brothers about it. Listen to the response of Shem and Japheth (Noah's other two sons) when they heard what had happened:

> *22 And Ham, the father of Canaan, saw the nakedness of his father and told his two brothers outside. 23 Then Shem and Japheth took a garment, laid it on both their shoulders, and walked backward and covered the nakedness of their father. Their faces were turned backward, and they did not see their father's nakedness. (Genesis 9)*

Shem and Japheth, placing a garment on their shoulders, walked backwards and covered the nakedness of their father. In doing so they did not see their father's naked body. They respected their father by not looking at his nakedness. Notice the response of Noah to his sons when he discovered what had happened:

> 24 When Noah awoke from his wine and knew what
>   his youngest son had done to him, 25 he said,
>
> "Cursed be Canaan;
> a servant of servants shall he be to his brothers."
>
> 26 He also said,
> "Blessed be the Lord, the God of Shem;
> and let Canaan be his servant.
> 27 May God enlarge Japheth,
> and let him dwell in the tents of Shem,
> and let Canaan be his servant." (Genesis 9)

Noah cursed his son Ham and his descendants for seeing his nakedness and not covering him up. He blessed Shem and Japheth, however, because they refused to look at his nakedness.

When Adam and Eve were in the Garden of Eden, they were naked and not ashamed (see Genesis 2:25). When they sinned, however, things changed. In Genesis 3:7 we read:

> 7 Then the eyes of both were opened, and they
> knew that they were naked. And they sewed fig
> leaves together and made themselves loincloths.

(Genesis 3)

Life would never again be the same for Adam and Eve. With the entrance of sin came lustful and shameful thoughts. From that moment forward, they covered themselves. In fact, God Himself made clothes to cover their nakedness:

> *21 And the LORD God made for Adam and for his wife garments of skins and clothed them (Genesis 3)*

The apostle Paul challenged women of his day to dress modestly:

> *9 likewise also that women should adorn themselves in respectable apparel, with modesty and self-control, not with braided hair and gold or pearls or costly attire, 10 but with what is proper for women who profess godliness—with good works. (1 Timothy 2)*

The apostle is not saying that women should never braid their hair or wear jewellery. These things are fine in themselves. What Paul is saying, however, is that we need to be modest, respectful and self-controlled in how we dress.

Modesty is the attitude of someone who is free from the need to seek attention. Self-control is the attitude of one who dresses with his or her sexual and emotional passions in check.

The priests of the Old Testament were to be careful in how they ministered. Exodus 20:26 tells us:

> *25 If you make me an altar of stone, you shall not build it of hewn stones, for if you wield your tool on it you profane it. 26 And you shall not go up by steps to my altar, that your nakedness be not exposed on it.' (Exodus 20)*

God required that any altar that was made for Him be low to the ground so that the priest would not have to climb steps to make their sacrifice. The reason for this was so that people below the altar would not have to see the nakedness of the priest on the steps offering the sacrifice. This would not only be distracting in worship but dishonour the priest who was performing his duty.

What we learn here is that Scripture challenges us to be modest in our dress and appearance, respecting not only ourselves but those around us. Like Job, we need to make a covenant with our eyes not to allow anything into our lives that would defile our hearts, minds and bodies with sinful thoughts and actions. The images, words and pictures we see around us can cause us to sin in our hearts and minds. We need to become aware of these triggers and turn from them for our own good and the glory of God.

For Consideration:

How much influence does pornography have in your society? What has been the result?

What is the connection between pornography and lust?

Is it a sin to lust even if you don't act on that lust? Explain.

Job made a covenant with his eyes not to gaze on a young virgin. What does it mean to make a covenant with one's eyes? Is this something that you need to do?

Paul tells us that as believers we need to dress modestly, with respect and self-control. What is the attitude of the person who dresses this way? Is this your attitude?

For Prayer:

Have you ever struggled with pornography? Ask the

Lord to give you victory over this.

Ask the Lord to give you a desire to be sexually pure in mind and attitude.

Do you know someone who has become trapped by pornography? Take a moment to pray that the Lord would help them to overcome and walk in purity of heart and mind.

Ask the Lord to give you strength like Job to make a covenant with your eyes not to look lustfully at another person.

Ask the Lord to give you grace to be faithful to your husband or wife not just physically but also in mind and heart.

15 - CELIBACY

In Genesis 2:18 we read:

18 Then the Lord God said, "It is not good that the man should be alone; I will make him a helper fit for him." (Genesis 2)

God created within us a need for companionship. Though Adam enjoyed the presence of God in the Garden of Eden, there was still a need within him for someone like him with whom he could share his life. The "helper" God created for Adam was a woman. Together they would compliment each other and satisfy this need of companionship.

Adam and Eve would form a life-long bond of faithfulness and raise a family. This was not always easy. In fact, there were deep struggles in their relationship. Adam had to work hard to provide for his family. Eve experienced deep pain in bringing her children into the world. Cain, their son would kill his brother in the first murder in history bringing deep grief to their heart.

One day the Pharisees asked Jesus if a man could divorce his wife for any reason (Matthew 19:3):

> *3 And Pharisees came up to him and tested him by asking, "Is it lawful to divorce one's wife for any cause?" (Matthew 19)*

Jesus responded by saying: "What therefore God has joined together, let no man separate" (Matthew 19:6). Hearing His answer, the disciples said:

> *10 ... "If such is the case of a man with his wife, it is better not to marry." (Matthew 19)*

The answer Jesus gave to this question is important:

> *11 But he said to them, "Not everyone can receive this saying, but only those to whom it is given. 12 For there are eunuchs who have been so from birth, and there are eunuchs who have been made eunuchs by men, and there are eunuchs who have made themselves eunuchs for the sake of the kingdom of heaven. Let the one who is able to receive this receive it." (Matthew 19)*

Let's take a moment to examine what Jesus is saying in Matthew 19:11-12. He told His disciples that the ability to live without a husband or wife was only given to certain people. He lists three different types of people here in verse 12 who have been given this ability.

First, Jesus speaks about those who have been born eunuchs. The word "eunuch" in the Greek language is "eunouchos". This word comes from two other words. The first part of the word comes from the Greek word "eune" which refers to a bed. The second word, "echo", has the sense of keeping or holding onto something. When the two words are put together they carry the meaning of a person who holds his bed for himself. In other words, he sleeps alone. He is not in a sexual relationship. According to Jesus, some people are born eunuchs. There can be several reasons for this. Some are born with physical or mental disabilities and may be incapable of marrying and having a family.

Second, according to Jesus, there are those who have been made eunuchs by man. In some cases, the male sex organ was cut off. Deuteronomy 23 recognizes this group when it says:

1 No one who testicles are crushed or whose male organ is cut off shall enter the assembly of the LORD. (Deuteronomy 23)

Finally, there were individuals who chose to remain single. This may have been to give themselves fully to the calling of God in their lives. The apostle Paul, for example, chose to be single and devote his entire life to the ministry God had given him.

What Jesus told His disciples that day was that there are people who chose, for whatever reason, never to marry. To these individuals Jesus said: "Let the one who is able to receive this receive it" (Matthew 19:12). In other words, if you feel that you want to remain single then you have the blessing of the Lord.

As we have already mentioned, the apostle Paul chose not to marry. As a single man, Paul celebrated his singleness but also encouraged marriage for those who did not have this ability. Listen to what he said to the Corinthians:

> *1 Now concerning the matters about which you wrote: "It is good for a man not to have sexual relations with a woman." 2 But because of the temptation to sexual immorality, each man should have his own wife and each woman her own husband. 3 The husband should give to his wife her conjugal rights, and likewise the wife to her husband. (1 Corinthians 7)*

Paul told the Corinthians that it was good for a man not to have a sexual relationship with a woman.

Understanding that not every man or woman could live without a sexual relationship, however, Paul encouraged marriage. Not only did he encourage marriage, but he urged husbands and wives to meet each other's sexual needs lest they fall into temptation.

Paul would go on to say:

> *6 Now as a concession, not a command, I say this. 7 I wish that all were as I myself am. But each has his own gift from God, one of one kind and one of another. 8 To the unmarried and the widows I say that it is good for them to remain single, as I am. 9 But if they cannot exercise self-control, they should marry. For it is better to marry than to burn with passion (1 Corinthians 7)*

Paul encouraged believers to consider remaining single but recognized that not everyone had the ability to do so. In 1 Corinthians 7:7 the apostle speaks of celibacy or singleness as a "gift from God." Obviously, Paul had this gift and devoted his entire life to the service of God. He recognized, however, that sexual passion was very strong in some individuals and they needed to be married.

According to Paul, those who marry have obligations and troubles in this life:

> *28 But if you do marry, you have not sinned, and if a betrothed woman marries, she has not sinned. Yet those who marry will have worldly troubles, and I would spare you that. (1 Corinthians 7)*

While marriage was honourable, it was not trouble-free. In fact, Paul reminds those who want to marry that they will have "worldly troubles." Those worldly troubles come in many forms. Paul explains this further in 1 Corinthians 7:32-34:

> *32 I want you to be free from anxieties. The unmarried man is anxious about the things of the Lord, how to please the Lord. 33 But the married man is anxious about worldly things, how to please his wife, 34 and his interests are divided. And the unmarried or betrothed woman is anxious about the things of the Lord, how to be holy in body and spirit. But the married woman is anxious about worldly things, how to please her husband. (1 Corinthians 7)*

The married man is obligated to his wife and family. He must do all he can to provide for their needs. He must have time with them to minister to them in their pain and struggles. This means that his "interests are divided" (verse 34). By marrying, this man increases his anxiety and concern. He is concerned for his wife and his children and his relationship with them. All this requires an expenditure of money, effort and time. He is not as free to do as he pleases. He must make sacrifices. He must be more disciplined in the use of his time. He financial costs are greater than that of a single man. He cannot be involved in as many voluntary projects or ministries as the single man. He will not have the same amount of time for the Lord as a single person. For Paul, this was a sacrifice that a married man or woman had to make and one that needed careful consideration before choosing to be married.

Paul's word of advice to the Corinthians in 1 Corinthians 7:35 is this:

> *35 I say this for your own benefit, not to lay any restraint upon you, but to promote good order and to secure your undivided devotion to the Lord. 36 If anyone thinks that he is not behaving properly toward his betrothed, if his passions are strong, and it has to be, let him do as he wishes: let them marry—it is no sin. 37 But whoever is firmly established in his heart, being under no necessity but having his desire under control, and has determined this in his heart, to keep her as his betrothed, he will do well. 38 So then he who marries his betrothed does well, and he who refrains from marriage will do even*

better. (1 Corinthians 7)

To men or women whose "passions are strong" Paul says: "let them marry—it is no sin" (verse 36). But to those who have their "desire under control" and choose not to marry, they did well (verse 37). Paul believed that the person who remained single was happier than the one who was married (verse 38).

> *39 A wife is bound to her husband as long as he lives. But if her husband dies, she is free to be married to whom she wishes, only in the Lord. 40 Yet in my judgment she is happier if she remains as she is. And I think that I too have the Spirit of God. (1 Corinthians 7)*

Paul is not commanding singleness. He encouraged marriage but challenges those who marry to understand that they will have struggles that the single person would not have. They would not be as free to serve or spend time with the Lord as the single person.

Celibacy is a gift from God that enables a person to remain single and focused on the task given to them by God without the distractions of a family. It enables that person to focus his or her resources on the calling of God. It gives them more time with the Lord. Before choosing to marry, Paul challenged the believer to consider whether celibacy is a gift and calling on their life.

For Consideration:

If you are married, what sacrifices and obligations do you have that a single person does not have?

What is the gift of celibacy? How can this be described as a gift? Do you have this gift? How can you use it for the glory of God?

What does this chapter teach us about the power of sexual desire? Is everyone able to remain single?

What cultural pressure is placed on those who want to remain single?

What are the advantages of celibacy?

For Prayer:

If you are married ask the Lord to help you to take your obligations and responsibilities toward your wife and family seriously.

If you are single, ask the Lord to show you whether He would have you to be married or if He has a purpose for you as a single person.

Do you know a single person who is wanting to be married but cannot find a partner? Take a moment to pray for this individual, asking God to make His will known.

Take a moment to pray for single believers in your church, whether they are widows, widowers or never married. Ask God to bless and encourage them in the path they are walking.

16 - SEXUAL DESIRE IN MARRIAGE

As we have been examining the teaching of Scripture about human sexuality we have considered a variety of forbidden relationships. In the last chapter, we saw what the apostle Paul taught about the gift of celibacy. It might be easy to assume from this that sexual relations are a necessary evil to populate the earth. In this chapter, however, I would like to take a moment to examine the teaching of Scripture about sexual desire in marriage. The Bible has much to say about the enjoyment of this relationship in marriage.

In Genesis 26, Isaac and his wife Rebekah traveled to Gerar where they met King Abimelech of the Philistines. Because Rebekah was a beautiful woman

(Genesis 26:7), Isaac feared that the king would kill him and take her to be his wife. Together they decided to deceive Abimelech by telling him that Rebekah was his sister. It was the hope that the king would then treat them well. As the story unfolds, we read in Genesis 26:8-9:

> *8 When he had been there a long time, Abimelech king of the Philistines looked out of a window and saw Isaac laughing with Rebekah his wife. 9 So Abimelech called Isaac and said, "Behold, she is your wife. How then could you say, 'She is my sister'?" Isaac said to him, "Because I thought, 'Lest I die because of her.'" (Genesis 26)*

There are a couple of details we need to see in these verses. Abimelech saw Isaac "laughing with" Rebekah. Consider how the phrase "laughing with" is translated in other versions of the Bible:

"showing endearment" – New King James Version
"fondling" – New Living Translation
"caressing" – New International Version

The idea here is that they were enjoying each other.

Notice that when King Abimelech saw what was happening between Isaac and Rebekah, he understood that they were married. What they were doing, obviously, was something that only a married couple would do. The English Standard Version translation ("laughing with") suggests that this caressing, fondling or showing of endearment brought joy to the couple.

The Bible encourages couples to rejoice or take great joy in each other. As Solomon reflected on the purpose and meaning of life, he challenged married couples to enjoy life with each other:

> *9 Enjoy life with the wife whom you love, all the days of your vain life that he has given you under the sun, because that is your portion in life and in your toil at which you toil under the sun. (Ecclesiastes 9)*

In fact, the prophet Isaiah speaks of the love of God for His people and compares it to that of a bride and bridegroom:

> *4 You shall no more be termed Forsaken,*
> *and your land shall no more be termed Desolate,*
> *but you shall be called My Delight Is in Her,*
> *and your land Married;*
> *for the Lord delights in you,*
> *and your land shall be married.*
> *5 For as a young man marries a young woman,*
> *so shall your sons marry you,*
> *and as the bridegroom rejoices over the bride,*
> *so shall your God rejoice over you. (Isaiah 62)*

According to Isaiah, God would marry and take great delight in Israel. Just as a young man rejoices over his bride, so God would delight in His people. This delighting of the bride and the bridegroom in each other is seen in a very positive light. In fact, it reflects the relationship God wants with His people.

Listen to the command of Scripture to husbands in Proverbs 5:18-19:

18 Let your fountain be blessed,
and rejoice in the wife of your youth,
19 a lovely deer, a graceful doe.
Let her breasts fill you at all times with delight;
be intoxicated always in her love. (Proverbs 5)

The writer begins by saying "let your fountain be blessed". The use of the word "fountain" is connected to the context of the chapter. Here the writer is speaking about the dangers of adultery. In Proverbs 5:15 he calls for men to drink water from their own cistern. In other words, they were to be faithful and satisfy their sexual needs with their own wife. The writer describes the relationship of a husband and wife to a "fountain." A fountain is a constant and abundant source of flowing water that refreshes and satisfies. In this context it refers to their sexual relationship, which is like a constant fountain, satisfying their needs and desires. Notice that the writer blessed this "fountain". It is the desire of God that the sexual relationship of the married couple be a fountain of delight and satisfaction. In such a relationship, there would be no need or desire to look to anyone else.

The writer goes on in verse 18 to challenge the husband to rejoice in the wife of his youth. The idea is that he was to be glad and happy with his wife. He was to enjoy her presence. In verse 19 we see that this rejoicing was also to be sexual in nature. He was to let her breasts fill him with delight. He challenges the husband to be intoxicated in her love.

Probably the greatest example of the delighting of a husband and wife in each other is found in the Song of Solomon. In Song of Solomon 4, the husband takes a moment to describe his beloved. His description of her charm and beauty is quite detailed in the opening section of chapter 4. What is important for us to notice is his response to her and this beauty he sees in her:

> *9 You have captivated my heart, my sister, my bride;*
> *you have captivated my heart with one glance of your eyes,*
> *with one jewel of your necklace.*
> *10 How beautiful is your love, my sister, my bride!*
> *How much better is your love than wine,*

and the fragrance of your oils than any spice!
11 Your lips drip nectar, my bride;
honey and milk are under your tongue;
the fragrance of your garments is like the
fragrance of Lebanon. (Song of Solomon 4)

Solomon describes his bride as one who has captivated his heart (verse 9). With a single glance from her his heart was attracted to her. Her lips and tongue dripped honey and milk –they were sweet and satisfying to him and delighted him more than the finest of wine. In each other they found great satisfaction and pleasure.

In Song of Solomon 4:12-15, the husband compares his bride to a fruitful garden with the choicest of fruits and spices.

12 A garden locked is my sister, my bride,
a spring locked, a fountain sealed.
13 Your shoots are an orchard of pomegranates
with all choicest fruits,
henna with nard,
14 nard and saffron, calamus and cinnamon,
with all trees of frankincense,
myrrh and aloes,
with all choice spices—
15 a garden fountain, a well of living water,
and flowing streams from Lebanon. (Song of
Solomon 4)

His lover is a garden filled with wonderful smells, aromas and satisfying streams of living water.

While the groom delights in his bride, the bride also delights in her bridegroom. Notice her response to him in verses 16-17:

> *16 Awake, O north wind,*
> *and come, O south wind!*
> *Blow upon my garden,*
> *let its spices flow.*
> *Let my beloved come to his garden,*
> *and eat its choicest fruits. (Song of Solomon 4)*

In Song of Solomon 4 the husband spoke of the attractive aroma of his wife's spices and delicious fruit. He compares her to a beautiful garden. Notice here in Song of Solomon 4:16 how his wife now calls for the wind to blow from her garden. In other words, she wants her husband to smell the attractive aroma of her perfume. She pleads with him to come to her garden and eat its choicest fruits. She offers herself to her husband. Notice the response of the husband to her invitation in Song of Solomon 5:1:

> *1 I came to my garden, my sister, my bride,*
> *I gathered my myrrh with my spice,*
> *I ate my honeycomb with my honey,*
> *I drank my wine with my milk. (Song of Solomon*

5)

The husband comes to his garden (his bride) and enjoys her spices and honey.

While there are many passages in the Song of Solomon that depict the delight this couple has in each other, let me site just one more example. In Song of Solomon 7:6-10 we again catch a glimpse of this intense sexual desire the couple has for each other:

> *6 How beautiful and pleasant you are,*
> *O loved one, with all your delights!*
> *7 Your stature is like a palm tree,*
> *and your breasts are like its clusters.*
> *8 I say I will climb the palm tree*
> *and lay hold of its fruit.*
> *Oh may your breasts be like clusters of the vine,*
> *and the scent of your breath like apples,*
> *9 and your mouth like the best wine.*

> *She*
> *It goes down smoothly for my beloved,*
> *gliding over lips and teeth.*
> *10 I am my beloved's,*
> *and his desire is for me. (Song of Solomon 7)*

As chapter 7 begins, the husband speaks of his wife

as being very beautiful and pleasant. He reminds her that he loves her and delights in her. In verse 7 he describes her as being tall and slender like a palm tree. He compares her breasts to clusters of dates. He expresses his desire to climb this palm tree and take hold of its fruit. The implications are quite clear. He wants to make love to her. He wants to touch her and hold her. He compares her mouth to the best wine.

Notice her response in verses 9-10. When he compared her mouth to wine, she told him that this wine went down smoothly, gliding over her lips and teeth. She was pleased with his love and desire for her. While there are more examples of this healthy sexual desire in marriage, what I have cited is enough to show that Scripture speaks unashamedly of sexual desire in the context of a marriage.

As we move into the New Testament, the apostle Paul, who encouraged celibacy, also encouraged sexual intimacy in a married relationship. He went even further than this however, reminding husbands and wives of their obligation to minister to one another sexually:

> *3 The husband should give to his wife her conjugal rights, and likewise the wife to her husband. 4 For the wife does not have authority over her own body, but the husband does. Likewise the husband does not have authority over his own body, but the wife does. 5 Do*

not deprive one another, except perhaps by agreement for a limited time, that you may devote yourselves to prayer; but then come together again, so that Satan may not tempt you because of your lack of self-control. (1 Corinthians 7)

Notice what the apostle Paul is saying here. He tells husbands and wives that they were not to withhold a sexual relationship from their partner. The Greek word translated in verse 5 by "deprive" is the word "apostereo". It is defined as follows:

To deprive, wrong, or defraud another of what belongs to him. (Zodhiates, Spiros, AMG Complete Word Study Dictionary of the New Testament, "Apostereo" Cedar Rapids: Laridian)

There are two reasons why the husband and wife were not to deprive each other of a sexual relationship. The first was that their bodies did not belong to themselves. When they married they surrendered themselves to each other, giving each other the right their bodies. The second reason for not depriving each other was because of the nature of temptation to sexual sin and the desire of Satan to wear down and cause a believer, whose sexual desire is not satisfied, to fall into the temptation of lust and sexual sin.

It is quite clear from this that the sexual relationship is not just for producing children but also to minister to one another and satisfy sexual and emotional needs. We have been created with sexual desires and needs. Those needs, and desires are not wrong. In fact, Scripture encourages them in the context of a committed relationship. Paul commands husband and wives to be aware of each other's needs and to care for each other. The writer of Proverbs compares a marriage to a fountain – a constant supply of life and refreshing. May the Lord give us grace to be this for our spouses.

For Consideration:

From what we have seen in this chapter, is sex in marriage only for producing children?

What evidence is there in Genesis of Isaac and Rebekah "enjoying" a physical (sexual) relationship?

What does the Song of Solomon show us about the physical and sexual attraction between a couple?

In Isaiah 62:5 God compares His relationship with the nation of Israel to the rejoicing of a bridegroom in his bride. What does this comparison tell us about God's view of marriage?

Why is sex in marriage important according to Paul in 1 Corinthians 7:3-5?

Are you married? Are your sexual needs being fulfilled in your marriage? The writer of Proverbs compares a marriage to a fountain of living water. Is this how you would describe how you are for your partner? Are you a constant source of abundant encouragement and blessing emotionally and sexually?

For Prayer:

Thank the Lord that He has provided a means by which our sexual needs can be satisfied? Thank Him that these needs are legitimate in His eyes.

Have you been a fountain of blessing to your partner? If not, ask that Lord to open your heart to him or her in a new way.

Have you struggled with unsatisfied sexual and emotional needs? Ask the Lord to give you strength in these times. Pray that He would keep you from temptation even when those needs are not being satisfied.

Ask the Lord to bring healing and renewal to your sexual relationship with your partner. Thank the Lord for your partner. Ask Him to renew your delight and desire for each other.

17 - TEMPTATIONS AND FORGIVENESS

As I write, I am aware that we live in a fallen world. All of us have fallen short of the standard God has set out for our sexual lives in one way or another. We have all faced temptations. Some who read this may even wonder how the Lord could forgive them for our failures. Let me take a moment to conclude this study with a few words about temptation and forgiveness.

Temptation

In Genesis 39 we have of the relationship between Joseph and Potiphar's wife:

6 ... Now Joseph was handsome in form and appearance. 7 And after a time his master's wife cast her eyes on Joseph and said. "Lie with me." (Genesis 39)

This request of Potiphar's wife was not a one-time request. Genesis 39:10 tells us that "she spoke to Joseph day after day," asking him to sleep with her. Each time Joseph refused. The day came when she physically grabbed Joseph by his garment. On that occasion, Joseph slipped out of his coat and ran away:

11 But one day, when he went into the house to do his work and none of the men of the house was there in the house, 12 she caught him by his garment, saying, "Lie with me." But he left his garment in her hand and fled and got out of the house. (Genesis 39)

Joseph was in a very difficult situation. Day after day he was in contact with Potiphar's wife who kept asking him to sleep with her. His job required him to be at the home of this woman. Imagine what Joseph was going through in those days. He wanted to be faithful to God and his master, but he was being tempted day after day.

While Joseph was tempted by Potiphar's wife, he did

not sin. In a similar way, the Lord Jesus was tempted by Satan, but did not sin. In fact, the writer to the Hebrews tells us that it was because Jesus was tempted like we are that He can truly understand our needs:

> *15 For we do not have a high priest who is unable to sympathize with our weaknesses, but one who in every respect has been tempted as we are, yet without sin. (Hebrews 4)*

The phrase "tempted yet without sin" is significant. It shows us that temptation is not a sin. Sin comes when we yield to temptation. Why is it important that we understand this? All too many of us feel defeated because we have been tempted. Let me be clear here, while temptation is not a sin, it can very quickly turn into lust or physical sin. The key is not to let it get to that point. Joseph left his garment in the hands of Potiphar's wife and fled the scene before he surrendered to temptation. This is what we need to do. We must recognize the temptations Satan throws on our path and turn from them before they cause us to fall.

As Christians, it is our desire and obligation to follow the teaching of Scripture. We will be tempted. For some, that temptation will be to lust after another person's spouse. For others, it will be to engage in sexual activity with a member of the same sex. What will we do with these temptations? Will you choose to walk in God's purpose or will you surrender? We only fail when we surrender to the temptations physically or emotionally. For many, the temptation will be an ongoing battle. A recovering alcoholic may have to battle with their desire for alcohol for the rest of their life. Alcoholics can live in victory over these temptations, however, by refusing to yield to their cravings. This is also true for sexual sins. The goal for us as believers, is to walk faithfully with the Lord and in His purpose for our sexual lives. For those who truly want to walk in God's purpose, the apostle Paul promise that God will give them strength to walk in victory:

13 No temptation has overtaken you that is not common to man. God is faithful, and he will not let you be tempted beyond your ability, but with the temptation he will also provide the way of escape, that you may be able to endure it. (1 Corinthians 10)

This world in which we live is affected tremendously by sin. This sin touches our bodies and minds. It affects our hearts and our sexual desires. We will be tempted and even struggle day after day with temptations just like Joseph. Will we choose, however, to walk in victory like him. For all who will commit themselves to God and His purpose, Scripture promises that God's grace will be enough

(2 Corinthians 12:8) and that "he will provide a way of escape" (1 Corinthians 10:13). Let us trust this promise in our time of need.

Forgiveness

Not everyone walks in the purpose of God. In our marriages, we have often become selfish or failed to live as one flesh with our partner. For some pre-marital sexual relations or homosexuality have been in their past. Lust and pornography have entrapped others. These sins continue to haunt some people. They feel unclean and wonder how God could ever forgive them.

These sins have left scars in the lives of those who have been affected. Victims of rape or sexual abuse often struggle for the rest of their lives with the memory of what took place. Adultery can have deep seated consequences for a marriage. Pornography and lust can rewire the brain. Children born out of wedlock may struggle to understand why their father or mother abandoned them. These are the consequences of sexual sin. The direction of our lives can change because of these sins. We may never undo the hurt our sexual sins have caused, we must learn to live with these consequences.

While our lives can change because of sin, there is also forgiveness for our actions. Jesus forgave the woman caught in the act of adultery in John 8 saying:

10 ... Woman, where are they? Has no one condemned you?" 11 She said, "No one, Lord." And Jesus said, "Neither do I condemn you; go, and from now on sin no more." (John 8)

The Old Testament demanded the death penalty for adultery but in Christ there is forgiveness.

When Jesus was in the home of a Pharisee in Luke 7, a prostitute came in and washed his feet with her tears. Seeing her repentant heart, Jesus said to her, "Your sins are forgiven" (Luke 7:48). While those present that day resented this, Jesus told her that her faith had saved her. She would leave His presence in peace with God.

David, who committed adultery with Bathsheba was forgiven when he repented and become Israel's greatest king. He would be described as a man after God's own heart (Acts 13:22).

Writing to the Corinthians the apostle Paul would say:

9 Or do you not know that the unrighteous will not inherit the kingdom of God? Do not be deceived: neither the sexually immoral, nor idolaters, nor adulterers, nor men who practice homosexuality, 10 nor thieves, nor the greedy, nor drunkards, nor revilers, nor swindlers will inherit the kingdom of God. 11 And such were some of you. But you were washed, you were sanctified, you were justified in the name of the Lord Jesus Christ and by the Spirit of our God. (1 Corinthians 6)

For our purpose in this study, notice the sexual sins listed here in this passage. Paul speaks of those who were sexually immoral, adulterers and those who practice homosexuality. The apostle understood that some of the Corinthians engaged in these evil practices (verse 11). Those who had been sexually immoral, adulterers and practiced homosexuality, were now washed and sanctified. They were brought into a relationship with Jesus Christ and forgiven of their sins. While the Old Testament law called for the death of those who practiced such sexual sins, the New Testament offered cleansing and forgiveness for all who came to the Lord Jesus.

The apostle John would put it this way:

7 But if we walk in the light, as he is in the light, we have fellowship with one another, and the blood of Jesus his Son cleanses us from all sin. 8 If we say we have no sin, we deceive ourselves, and the truth is not in us. 9 If we confess our sins, he is faithful and just to forgive us our sins and to cleanse us from all unrighteousness. (1 John 1)

Notice what the apostle tells us in these verses. He reminds us that the blood of Jesus "cleanses us from all sin" (verse 7). He tells us that if we confess our sin, the Lord God is faithful to "cleanse us from all unrighteousness" (verse 9). Sexual sins are no exception. For those who have fallen short of God's standard, the call of Scripture is to seek Christ and the forgiveness He offers.

We are living in an age that does not value the purpose of God for human sexuality. Our society has not only accepted expressions of sexuality that are contrary to the teaching of the Bible, but it has also made it a crime to speak out against these practices. The church of our day has also been affected by this. Moral failure among pastors and church leaders has become obvious. We are seeing an increasing number of sexual problems in churches of our day. It is because of this that I felt the leading of the Lord to prepare this study. I have not covered every aspect of human sexuality in this study. The issues I have addressed in this study, however, are laid out quite clearly for us in the Bible.

As believers, we are not to be governed by what society tells us. Our authority for life and practice is the Word of God. My attempt in this study has been to survey the teaching of Scripture about human sexuality. My challenge to every believer reading this study, is to make it his or her commitment to walk in obedience to God's purpose for their sexuality. God has created us as sexual beings. Sexual relationships are for the enjoyment and blessing of a married couple. These relationships, however, are to be enjoyed only in the context of a committed relationship between a man and a wife.

Will you make it your commitment to surrender your sexuality to the Lord God? Will you devote yourself to walking in His purpose? Will you resist every temptation that comes your way? Will you seek to grow in your understanding of your sexual relationship with your husband or wife? In our day, we see a free and unashamed expression of human sexuality. We are bombarded on every side by these expressions. May God give us grace, however, to walk as He intended. May we be an example of God's purpose for our society.

For Consideration:

Is temptation sin? What do we need to do with temptation?

What is the difference between sexual temptation and lust?

What promises does the Bible give to those who are tempted?

Is there forgiveness for sexual sin? Give some examples from Scripture.

Have you been living in victory over sexual temptations? What are your areas of weakness?

For Prayer:

Thank the Lord that He promises victory to those who turn to Him in their temptations. Ask the Lord to give you victory over the temptations you face.

If you are married, is your sexual relationship such that you are no longer being tempted by outside attractions? Are you causing your partner to stumble by sexual refusal?

Have you been guilty of sexual sin in the past? Ask the Lord to forgive and cleanse you. Thank Him that His grace covers all our sins.

Ask God to give you the strength and commitment necessary to live a pure and godly life. Surrender your sexual life to Him and ask for His blessing and strength to overcome any temptations in His name.

ABOUT THE AUTHOR

Light To My Path Book Distribution

Light To My Path Book Distribution (LTMP) is a book writing and distribution ministry reaching out to needy Christian workers in Asia, Latin America, and Africa. Many Christian workers in developing countries do not have the resources necessary to obtain Bible training or  purchase Bible study materials for their ministries and personal encouragement.

F. Wayne Mac Leod is a member of Action International Ministries and has been writing these books with a goal to distribute them freely or at cost price to needy pastors and Christian workers around the world. These books are being used in preaching, teaching, evangelism and encouragement of local believers in over sixty countries. Books have now been translated into a number of languages. The goal is to make them available to as many believers as possible.

The ministry of LTMP is a faith-based ministry and we trust the Lord for the resources necessary to distribute the books for the encouragement and strengthening of believers around the world. Would you pray that the Lord would open doors for the translation and further distribution of these books?

For more information about Light To My Path Book Distribution visit our website at www.lighttomypath.ca

www.ingramcontent.com/pod-product-compliance
Lightning Source LLC
Chambersburg PA
CBHW050909260726

48660CB00001B/111